In Search of Adolescence takes on the revisionist history so widely accepted in the Church and the broader culture—the "history" that portrays adolescence itself as a modern invention, an aberration of the way young people were meant to grow up. A winsome writer, a fearless academic, and a brilliant researcher, Crystal Kirgiss unmasks the simplistic assumptions we've held for so long about the nature and importance of adolescence. Like a sharpshooter in a carnival shooting gallery, Crystal's book blows away falsehood after falsehood with perfectly aimed research and totally disarming humor. This book has the potential to make us totally rethink the way we see young people and our work with them.

Mark DeVries, MDiv | @markdevriesYMA
Founder, Ministry Architects
Author of *Sustainable Youth Ministry*

Crystal Kirgiss lays down the gauntlet: If we'd done our homework more carefully, maybe we wouldn't have swallowed the "adolescence-as-recent-social-construct" thesis so readily. With the temerity of a well-armed historian and the compassion of a long-time youth minister, Kirgiss turns conventional theories of childhood on their heads by arguing that adolescence has been around a lot longer than we think. Agree or disagree, *In Search of Adolescence* is a joyous read that turns one of youth ministry's most sacred cows into hamburger.

Kenda Creasy Dean, PhD | @kendacreasydean
Mary D. Synnott Professor of Youth, Church, and Culture
Princeton Theological Seminary
Author of *Almost Christian*

As foundational as the notion of adolescence is to the practice of youth ministry, few of us have had the training or done the work to dig into its history. Crystal Kirgiss serves us well in bringing to light how that stage between childhood and adulthood has been understood and addressed in the West for centuries. *In Search of Adolescence* provides solid research and reflective insight into how this season of life change has always been a contextual struggle—not only for the adolescents themselves but for parents, communities, and the Church—and what it means to encourage and care for those moving through this historically "normal" stage of life.

Chap Clark, PhD | @chapclark
Professor of Youth, Family, and Culture
Fuller Theological Seminary
Author of *Hurt 2.0*

Rarely do you find someone who is willing to go against the popular narrative the way Crystal Kirgiss does in this fantastic book. In it, she challenges long-held assumptions and helps carve out a new path for thinking about adolescence. This book truly is a gift to the youth worker community!

Kurt Johnston | @kurtjohnston
Pastor to Students, Saddleback Church
Author of *Middle School Ministry Made Simple*

For my entire adult life I've been working hard to figure out adolescents and adolescence. My growing collection of definitions and anecdotes regarding this in-between period indicates that both of the aforementioned tasks are like trying to nail Jell-O to a wall. Now, I owe a big thanks to Crystal Kirgiss for adding some significant research and ideas to my ongoing quest as a parent, youth worker, and youth culture analyst. *In Search of Adolescence* is a must-read for anyone longing to understand and reach our precious kids.

Walt Mueller, PhD | @CPYU
Founder and President, Center for Parent/Youth Understanding
Author of *Youth Culture 101*

This book is a much needed look at how adolescence has been understood throughout history. It's fascinating but, more importantly, it's an invitation to see adolescence in what may be a new way—not as a social construct, or a problem to be solved, or a stage to be endured, but as a precious phase of life, designed uniquely by God to reflect his image. For both young people and the adults who influence them, that's great news.

Elle Campbell | @ellllllllllle
Cofounder, StuffYouCanUse.org
Coauthor of *Creating a Lead Small Culture*

This is a rare book that will change the way we think and speak about adolescence. Crystal Kirgiss has mined the history of adolescence for captivating gems and social maps that are treasures to help us better understand young people today. This book is at the cutting edge of adolescent research, not just in youth ministry but across disciplines. The best part, though, is that Crystal's gifted writing makes it an easy and delightful read that will inspire us in all our work with youth.

Terry Linhart, PhD | @terrylinhart
Chair of the Dept. of Religion and Philosophy, Bethel College
Coauthor of *Global Ministry: Reaching Adolescents Around the World*

This book is smart. It's witty, down-to-earth, well-researched, and quite possibly ground-breaking. I have only one complaint: Reading *In Search of Adolescence* is forcing me to reconfigure or, at least, rethink pretty much everything I've been believing and teaching about adolescence over the last three decades! But the insights of this book are persuasive and profound. With a perfect mix of thorough scholarship and ministry passion Crystal—a seasoned youth ministry vet herself—offers a vital contribution to our understanding of adolescence and the way we minister to teenagers.

Duffy Robbins, DMin | @duffyrobbins
Professor of Youth Ministry, Eastern University
Author of *Building a Youth Ministry That Builds Disciples*

This book is a game changer for anyone who thinks that adolescence is a modern invention. Crystal Kirgiss' lively romp through the sometimes sordid, sometimes hilarious history of adolescence should spark an important conversation among parents, youth ministers, and youth ministry educators. We need to listen to her call to see young people for who they really are, rather than repeating misleading historical narratives that stereotype them.

Tom Bergler, PhD | @huntingtonu
Professor Ministry and Missions, Huntington University
Author of *The Juvenilization of American Christianity*

IN SEARCH OF
adolescence
A NEW LOOK AT AN OLD IDEA

BY CRYSTAL KIRGISS

THE YOUTH CARTEL

In Search of Adolescence

Copyright © 2015 by Crystal Kirgiss

Publisher: Mark Oestreicher
Managing Editor: Tamara Rice
Cover Design: Adam McLane
Layout: Marilee R. Pankratz
Creative Director: Juliet Capulet

ISBN-10: 1942145144
ISBN-13: 978-1-942145-14-1

The Youth Cartel, LLC
www.theyouthcartel.com
Email: info@theyouthcartel.com

Born in San Diego
Printed in the U.S.A.

To every adult who patiently and faithfully walked alongside me while I awkwardly traversed adolescence.

To every parent and youth worker who patiently and faithfully does the same for their adolescents.

To my husband, who has not only patiently and faithfully walked alongside countless teenagers while they traverse adolescence but also me while I traverse life. His consistent embodiment and reflection of the Savior's love is breathtaking.

Contents

INTRODUCTION

A few years ago, Mark Oestreicher invited me to speak about the history of adolescence at a Youth Cartel Summit. We had talked about my research on several different occasions over the years, and he thought it would be a good addition to that year's lineup.

There is perhaps nothing more potentially deflating than being asked to speak about h-i-s-t-o-r-y at the same event where David Crowder is scheduled to speak about creativity and Brad Montague is scheduled to speak about creating the Kid President videos. (Except maybe being asked to write about h-i-s-t-o-r-y for people who converse knowledgably and eloquently—and almost exclusively—about the twenty-first century.)

I set low expectations for the presentation. I even chopped my allotted fifteen minutes down to thirteen hoping the brevity would earn me some grace. I mean, *history*—at a youth worker shindig. Please.

Lo and behold, the history of adolescence wasn't received with the feigned polite *ho-hum* yawns that I expected. Quite the opposite. The audience leaned in. The debrief discussion was well attended. The follow-up conversations were animated.

I was rather surprised to what degree the topic struck a chord with so many people. I'd been writing and researching about adolescence in the Middle Ages for such a long time that it was old news to me. In fact, it was long past being any kind of news at all. It simply *was*. Besides, I had spent so many years being a Lone Ranger of sorts—a non-traditional academic who researches historical adolescence and a nonconventional youth worker who spends time with today's adolescents—that I'd grown quite used to being the only one who noticed or cared about the historical elements.

While preparing for the Summit, my research necessarily moved far past the Middle Ages and far beyond literary texts into all kinds of other source material. I had no agenda beyond that of finding everything I could about adolescence before 1800—give or take a century or so. It might have been helpful if someone had proof-texted Ecclesiastes 12:12 (NLT) for me back then:

> My child, let me give you some further advice: Be careful, for writing books is endless, and much study wears you out.

Wears you out indeed. But also fills you up. Revs your engine. Lights your fire. Brings you to life. *Blah, blah, blah.* It's near impossible to explain the neurological high that results from spending days upon days upon months upon years in the delightfully murky netherworlds known as Early English Books Online and Eighteenth-Century Collections Online. It's quite overwhelming, in every good way. (Ecclesiastes 12:12, though …)

Here is what I know today about the history of adolescence: There is so very much that we still do *not* know about the history of adolescence. Learning is like that sometimes. The more you know, the more you realize how much you don't know. That's both frustrating and exciting.

By a strange quirk of circumstances, an obsessive inclination to study the same literature that C. S. Lewis, J. R. R. Tolkien, and Dorothy Sayers studied, and the persistent encouragement of one friend in particular, this season of life has become a determined and delightful search for adolescence across a wide swath of historical eras. Many people—specifically those who claim that adolescence is a modern social and cultural construct—might deem this search pointless, futile, fruitless, and needless. At one time, I might have felt the same way. But not any longer. I'm more convinced than ever that it has significance and meaning far above and beyond my own imbalanced love for archival research.

It takes just one person clicking *return* and a millisecond of time to do a typical twenty-first-century search. Not so in this case. Recently, a number of people have been especially helpful in navigating and advancing this particular search:

Thomas Berndt (Psychological Sciences, Purdue University), Shaun Hughes (English, Purdue University), Melinda Zook (History, Purdue University), and Barbara Hanawalt (The Ohio State University, Emeritus) have given wise and learned interdisciplinary counsel;

Michael Johnston (English, Purdue University) graciously transcribed a folio of *Omne Bonum* while doing his own research at the British Library; Elizabeth Mercier (Classics, Purdue University) and Chad Judkins (PhD, Purdue University) promptly answered all of my tricky medieval Latin questions;

Kenda Creasy Dean (Princeton Theological Seminary), Andy Root (Luther Seminary), Tom Bergler (Huntington University), Terry Linhart (Bethel College, Mishawaka), Chap Clark (Fuller Theologicial Seminary), Duffy Robbins (Eastern University), Mark Devries (Ministry Architects), Walt Mueller (The Center for Parent and Youth Understanding), Marv Penner (All About Youth / National Center for Excellence in Youth Ministry), Chanon Ross (Institute for Youth Ministry), Jessicah Duckworth (Lilly Endowment), and Don Richter (Louisville Institute) have offered thoughtful feedback and insight into how this research might inform the continued study of adolescence and youth ministry;

Kurt Johnston (Saddleback Church), Scott Rubin (Willow Creek Community Church), and Mark Oestreicher (The Youth Cartel) have pondered with me what the practical implications of mountainous fusty historical information might be;

Tamara Rice (The Youth Cartel) has graciously maneuvered and managed my extended Ecclesiastes 12:12 showdown;

and Mark Kirgiss, youth worker *extraordinaire*, has reminded me about what really matters as he models faithful, persistent, and passionate youth ministry with impressive longevity and humble integrity.

IN SEARCH OF ADOLESCENCE | I

In my undergrad days, were I to go in search of adolescence as a paper topic for Developmental Psychology 101, I would march myself over to the college library, plant myself in front of the card catalog, pull the impossibly long drawer all the way out and start working my way from front to back, then spend some time riffling through the *Readers' Guide to Periodical Literature* until finally compiling a list of resources long enough to satisfy the syllabus requirements. Then would come the winding journey through row after row after row of bookshelves, a lengthy hunt for the elusive issues of academic journals stashed in every impossibly hidden location, a lengthy perusal through stacks and stacks of material, and painstaking note-taking on 3x5 cards that could later be sorted into some kind of coherent order.

Leg warmers, shoulder pads, big hair—and card catalogs. That pretty much sums up my '80s experience.

Fashion considerations aside, going in search of adolescence today is an entirely different adventure. With unlimited resources at our fingertips and with *search* taking on a whole new digital meaning, the collective sum of information is rather overwhelming. In just 0.36 seconds, even the laziest and least interested person can be the proud possessor of thirty-seven million hits of data about adolescence.

Lucky us. With all of that knowledge, we should be well on our way to having adolescence—all of life, in fact—figured out.

Indeed.

A few years ago, one of those thirty-seven million hits of data was a post from a syndicated blogger entitled: "Adolescence: A modern plague, but there is a cure."[1]

It started like this:

> Back in the old days, there were two types of people in the world: children and adults. You were a child and then you became an adult, and you really had no choice in the matter. The timeline of events went something like this:
>> Phase 1: Birth and childhood.
>> Phase 2: Adulthood.
>> Phase 3: Death.

The blogger then launched into a sweeping historical summary of adolescence, mixed with personal commentary, which included this:

> In modern Western society, we've delayed the onset of adulthood, instead inventing a new sort of human: the "teenager." The teenager exists in this limbo which we've created; we call it "adolescence." Adolescence is a state-

of-the-art modern innovation, like crack cocaine or chemical warfare.

This particular writer, who often tends toward hyperbole and sarcasm to make his point, put into words—albeit hyperbolically and sarcastically, seasoned with a dash of heightened pejorative alarm—what many of us have read, heard, or been taught, namely that adolescence is a recent social and cultural construct brought about by such things as the Industrial Revolution and extended public education. In other words, adolescence (it) is not natural or normal, which leads some people to conclude that adolescents (they) are not natural or normal either. This is a logical leap, apparently.

In the opinion of this particular blogger and others, adolescence goes far beyond being unnatural and abnormal. Devastatingly monstrous would be a better description. Maybe not quite so devastatingly monstrous as crack cocaine and chemical warfare, but pretty close.

While not everyone agrees with such a pejorative stance towards adolescence itself—thank goodness, else what hope would there be for the world?—most people agree with the historical framework within which this blogger presented his damning assessment, namely that there isn't one.

It's all new. It's all bad. It's all hopeless. And by *it*, they usually also mean *they*.

Crack cocaine. Chemical warfare. Lazy, insolent, disrespectful, full-of-themselves, know-it-all, moody, good-for-nothing bundles of hormones. You know the drill.

And so here we are, people who love adolescents and feel called to adolescent ministry, staring down the barrel of a frighteningly unnatural, abnormal, culturally constructed, non-divinely-designed stage of life.

Indeed.

That sounds promising.

REVISIONIST HISTORY

This notion of adolescence as a recent social and cultural construct—though not always wrapped in the stunningly judgmental sheen of the previously mentioned blogger—is presented as indisputable fact in a variety of places. It appears in science magazines, parenting books, developmental psychology roundtables, online reference sites, educational training materials, academic conferences, and youth ministry publications—many of which are reputable, wise, and practically useful.

It goes something like this:

> "In Europe and America, adolescence went largely unrecognized as a stage of life until the middle of the nineteenth century."[2]

> "Adolescence emerged as a distinct period in the lifespan under a number of unique social conditions at the advent of industrialism."[3]

> "Before the twentieth century adolescence was rarely included as a stage in the life cycle."[4]

> "Before the twentieth century young people in Western societies were thought of quite differently ... the notion of adolescence as a distinct stage of life was introduced

by social scientists at the turn of the century to name what was defined as a 'problem' created by young people."[5]

There is general agreement among sociologists and developmental psychologists that adolescence is new and that before the late nineteenth century there was not a recognized stage of life that came between childhood and adulthood. No transition. No in-between. No coming-of-age as a process. Therefore, statements like these are rarely questioned or challenged:

> "Before these ideas [i.e., adolescence and young adulthood] were invented, children were expected to take on adult roles as soon as they were able, apprenticing their parents and transitioning to adulthood with puberty."[6]

> "Many of the signers of the Declaration of Independence were still in their teens."[7]

Childhood. Adult roles. Puberty. Adulthood. Declaration of Independence.

It's all so very neat and tidy—but not true.

Before 1900, people were rarely awarded full adult rights and responsibilities at the onset of puberty. And not a single teenager signed the Declaration of Independence. The youngest signers were Thomas Lynch and Edward Rutledge, both age twenty-six, both lawyers. The average age was, in fact, forty-four.[8]

Many of the authors and researchers who make these statements do little more than present them before moving on to their main topic or issue. In some cases, the claims don't seem to have any implications or applications to their larger findings and theories. But in other cases, established assumptions about the "cultural invention of the social institution of adolescence" lead to broad-sweeping—and sometimes worrying—premises upon which to build various practices and enact public policies. One author connects the following dots:

> socially constructed adolescence leads to a false infantilization of teens
> false infantilization of teens leads to teen anger and depression
> teen anger and depression carries over into families and causes stress
> family stress leads to increased divorce rates

Summary: Higher divorce rates are at least partly a direct result of adolescence.[9]

Using this logic, negative elements of today's society that have either begun or increased since the late 1800s can all, with strategic maneuvering, be blamed on the "invention" of adolescence.

And so here we are once again, people who love adolescents and feel called to adolescent ministry, this time staring down the barrel of a life stage that is "not normal" to such a degree that it is the cause of various and sundry social ills.

Indeed.

If this were true, we might as well all go back to bed, pull the blankets over our heads, and refuse to come out until the whole world comes shattering down—which is probably going to happen if we don't hurry up and deconstruct, dismantle, and thoroughly obliterate the human-development version of crack cocaine and chemical warfare known as adolescence.

I hyperbolize.

Still, I don't think that starting from a place of inflated doom serves anyone, least of all those who are the supposed cause and source of said doom.

ARIÈS, HUMAN NATURE, AND THE NGRAM VIEWER

No one is entirely sure who first said that adolescence is a recent social construct. One likely possibility is that it all started with Philip Ariès whose book *Centuries of Childhood: A Social History of Family Life* made the bold claim that medieval society had absolutely "no idea of what we call adolescence." According to Ariès, Siegfried (from Richard Wagner's late nineteenth-century opera of the same name) was the first *real* adolescent (even though he was a fictionalized character living in a mythical world of Norse gods and dwarfs and dragons) because he displayed a "combination of purity, physical strength, naturism, spontaneity, and *joie de vivre* which was to make the adolescent the hero of our twentieth century, the century of adolescence."[10]

I suspect that Ariès had not read any medieval Arthurian tales, or Elizabethan ballads, or Colonial American law codes, or seventeenth-century sermons, or eighteenth-century picaresque novels. Else he surely would have known that Siegfried was certainly not the first character to display strong, natural, spontaneous, and *joie de vivre*-ish adolescence. Not by a long shot.

Though Ariès' influence continues to run deep, many of his

conclusions and research methods have been methodically reviewed and rejected in the last several decades by academic researchers.[11] But very few people in the worlds of adolescent development, sociology, psychology, or youth ministry are reading what those other researchers are writing.[12] We barely have enough time to read the books written in our own circles, let alone the books of other circles. That's one reason why this narrative about a recently socially constructed stage of life known as adolescence continues to maintain such persistent traction.

Human nature being what it is, we have a hard time letting go of our comfortable and firmly established narratives. This particular one runs quite deep in our collective youth ministry culture.

In a survey of 180 youth workers—almost 70% of whom had college degrees in youth ministry, human development, psychology, sociology, or education, and more than 80% of whom were paid youth workers[13]—respondents were asked to indicate which of the following statements were accurate, based on their understanding, education, training, or experience:

STATEMENT	% of respondents who agreed
Adolescence is a social construct.	66%
Adolescence has been a recognized stage of life for about 100 years.	60%
Adolescence resulted from various cultural shifts, including the Industrial Revolution and extended mandated education.	78%
Before the mid-1800s, people were viewed as either children or adults.	82%

Extended adolescence is a result of modern societal norms.	85%
None of the above.	4%

Respondents were then asked to identify which of the following were major sources of their knowledge about adolescence, specifically its recent cultural construction.

SOURCE	% of respondents who drew information from source
media portrayals	30%
college textbooks	38%
parenting books	44%
personal research	46%
college coursework	52%
youth ministry blogs	61%
seminars, workshops, conferences	78%
youth ministry books	80%

If someone were to ask what evidence there is for the recent social and cultural construction of adolescence—besides the textbooks, seminars, coursework, and blogs—the answers might include the following:

Everyone knows that people used to get married much younger than today.

And yet according to historical data, the average age of marriage in Colonial America was early twenties for females and mid-twenties for males, which was slightly lower than their European counterparts.[14]

Everyone knows that puberty used to start much later than today.

The truth is that puberty onset ages have *not* been in a steady decline, though they have perhaps fluctuated over time. In the Middle Ages, Hildegard of Bingen noted that girls were capable of reproduction as young as twelve.[15] A medical treatise from the later Middle Ages observed that puberty sometimes occurred earlier than the expected age of twelve to fourteen which the author attributed to better nutrition—or as he eloquently put it, "gluttony."[16]

Everyone knows that previous eras had many significant rites of passage that we lack today.

In fact, people who say this are often referring to knighthood, which was reserved for only *some* of the males. But what are such things as middle school graduation, Confirmation, getting a driver's license, high school prom, receiving one's first summer job paycheck, and high school graduation if not rites of passage? We may not have all the attendant pomp and revelry (themselves creations of our historical imaginations—and maybe also Disney) but no one can say we *don't* have rites of passage. Whether those rites have attendant meaning and value is another question entirely.

Everyone knows that people had adult responsibilities and lived wholly independent lives much younger than today, especially if they weren't part of the wealthy nobility who could afford a life of irresponsible leisure.

And yet apprentices could not engage in private commerce, join a guild, or marry until completing their contracted service, usually in the early to mid-twenties. Until then, they were tightly managed by the adult powers-that-be. Residents of early American colonies could not vote until age twenty-one. Ralph Josselin, a seventeeth-century diarist, left for school at age sixteen and returned home each time his debts ran up; left again at age twenty for an entry-level job and returned home when things didn't work out; obsessed over whether to work on his father's farm, study law, or go back to school; lived with his uncle when he was short on cash and opportunities until finally he became a tutor, then a schoolmaster, and then a member of the clergy. (Vocational ministry saves the day.)[17]

The word adolescent *wasn't known or used until the late nineteenth century. (Except for that one time in 1425.)*

And that time in 1439, and all those other times in the fifteenth, sixteenth, seventeenth, and eighteenth centuries. And that doesn't take into account the numerous Latin uses in medical, religious, and philosophical works in earlier centuries. The word *family* first appeared in 1452, defined as, "A group of people living as a household, traditionally consisting of parents and their children," and yet surely *family* was a known concept before that time.[18]

Even so, one sociologist put the power of the information age behind the argument. He tested the notion that adolescence was not merely discovered but actually invented at the turn of the twentieth century by running *adolescence* through the Google Ngram Viewer and posting the results on his website (results which were then picked up and posted on other websites).[19]

Here's what he came up with:

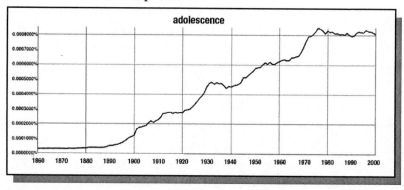

Results for *adolescence*. Philip N. Cohen, "The Appearance of the Invention of Adolescence," *Family Inequality* (blog), February 2011: https://familyinequality.wordpress.com/2011/02/02/the-appearance-of-the-invention-of-adolescence/. Reposted by Lisa Wade, "The Invention of 'Adolescence,' " *The Society Pages* (blog), February 2011: http://thesocietypages.org/socimages/2011/02/23/the-invention-of-adolescence/.

While I'm sure the Ngram Viewer can be an interesting source of information, we should be cautious about using it to either prove or disprove the existence of a concept, person, or thing. Else we would have to claim that there were no siblings until the early 1900s.

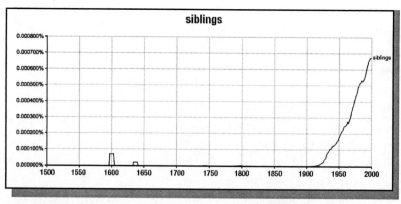

Results for *siblings*. https://books.google.com/ngrams/graph?content=siblings&year_start=1500&year end=2000&corpus=S15&smoothing=3&share=&direct_url=t1%3B%2Csiblings%3B%2Cc0

That means there were almost two centuries of single-child families, seeing as families weren't a major concept until after 1750 and didn't exist at all in the years just before and after 1700.

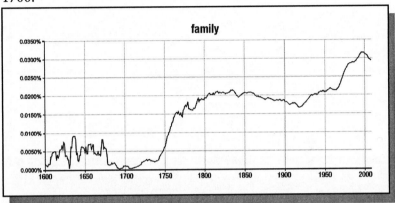

Results for *family*. https://books.google.com/ngrams/graph?content=family&year_start=1600&year_end=2008&corpus=15&smoothing=3&share=&direct_url=t1%3B%2Cfamily%3B%2Cc0

That might be because sex was essentially non-existent during those same years just before and after 1700.

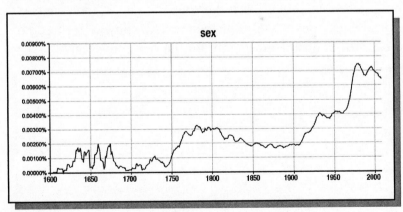

Results for *sex*. https://books.google.com/ngrams/graph?content=sex&year_start=1600&year_end=2008&corpus=15&smoothing=3&share=&direct_url=t1%3B%2Csex%3B%2Cc0

And that was probably because the devil was on a sabbatical of sorts at that time, according to the Ngram Viewer.[20]

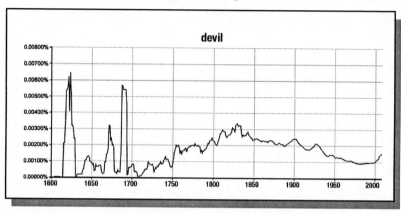

Results for *devil*. https://books.google.com/ngrams/graph?content=devil&year_start=1600&year_end=2008&corpus=15&smoothing=3&share=&direct_url=t1%3B%2Cdevil%3B%2Cc0

I jest. The point is that though lexical evidence might be entertaining for those who dabble in philology and linguistics, it is not necessarily the most reliable test of reality.

It is interesting, though, that the upward trend of adolescence from 1860 through 2000 coincided with the downward trend of the more populist word "youth" for the very same years.

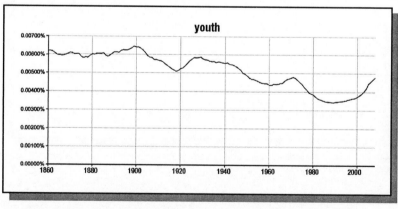

Results for *youth*. https://books.google.com/ngrams/graph?content=youth&year_start=1860&year_end=2008&corpus=15&smoothing=3&share=&direct_url=t1%3B%2Cyouth%3B%2Cc0

The sharp increase in the appearance of "adolescence" in printed material starting in 1900 is perhaps because in 1904, G. Stanley Hall's two-volume book titled *Adolescence: Its Psychology and Its Relations to Physiology, Anthropology, Sociology, Sex, Crime, Religion, and Education* swept onto the scene—just about the time when many people say adolescence was invented.[21] Hall's book was very big and very important. According to most experts, it marked the first time anyone had engaged in a serious study of the stage of life that bridged childhood and adulthood; it was, they say, the true birth of a brand new life stage, one that never before existed.

Like many others, I was on board with that.

But then along came the Squire. And the historians.

BACK TO CANTERBURY

I blame much of this on him—Chaucer's Squire, that is, one of the twenty-nine pilgrims traveling to the shrine of St. Thomas Becket in Canterbury. I first met him in my high school British Lit course, where he was just another pilgrim in just another book in just another unit in just another class that I needed to take in order to graduate.

Translation: I paid little attention.

Years later, I met him again in a graduate seminar, where he ran the very real risk of being just another character in just another Middle English dialect in just another canonical literary text that had to be analyzed through the lens of just another postmodern philosopher's verbose ramblings in order to earn my rank as a bona fide academic.

Translation: I lean towards "skeptical" in my views of literary critical theory.

As it happened, I was much older than my fellow graduate students and confidently comfortable in my middle-aged skin, so I was not afraid to set aside critical theory in favor of the stories as stories and the pilgrims as people; not the pilgrims as symbols of some profound and rhetorically philosophical meaning-of-life chatter, but just the pilgrims themselves. Plain old regular folk. Literarily fictive, but oh-so-realistically familiar.

People—even storied ones—are entirely mystifying and satisfying to contemplate. So I engaged in what my youth-ministry self might call "relational close reading." I spent time getting to know a cadre of colorful characters that defied their two-dimensional world of the printed page, much like youth pastors and teachers and parents and other interested adults get to know individual teens who defy their three-dimensional world of acculturated realities.

As I got to know those pilgrims better and better, the Squire— the youngest of the pilgrims and the only one whose age is given (he is "about twenty")—kept demanding my attention. While many of my colleagues saw oppressors, colonizers, subjects, objects, oppressed, and marginalized others (to name a few), I primarily saw the one and only *adolescent*.

While many of my colleagues were drawn to concerns of postcolonialism, Marxism, postmodernism, formalism, structuralism, feminism, new historicism, semiotics, gender, and psychoanalysis (to name a few), I found myself drawn to concerns of age, specifically *adolescence*.

While many of my colleagues went in search of the precursory shadows of Freud, Foucault, Derrida, Showalter, Leavis, Said, Barthes, Kristeva, Saussure, and Jameson (to name a few), I went in search of a young man who embodied adolescence and resembled many of the teenagers and young adults I had known over the years.

The Squire just wouldn't shut up, even though he says almost nothing (excluding his tale, that is, which is a rambling and tangled mess that perfectly exemplifies stereotypical youth trying to prove it already knows everything and is smarter by far than all the provincially dowdy adults the world can throw at it).

He just wouldn't go away, even though he did disappear most nights (like so many other stereotypical sex-crazed twenty-year-olds who stay up too late, getting no more sleep than a nightingale, because, you know, they are *busy*).

He just wouldn't kowtow to traditional adult behaviors and clothing, even though he is described as a good worker (still working for his own dad, by the way) who sports the latest hairstyle and outlandish fashions, notably tight hose (which would have made any modern pair of yoga pants look tame by comparison, leaving one to wonder how the tenuously righteous young women of that era were able to protect the purity of their hearts and guard the holiness of their minds).

It was all so utterly fascinating and eerily familiar. Aside from his archaic Middle English speech and his Spanx-like hose, the Squire could have been one of my college students, or a college-aged youth leader, or someone's grown-but-not-gone son. He was utterly contemporary, yet so very medieval.

Over and over again, I asked myself:

Why doesn't anyone pay attention to the Squire?

His tale gets a nod now and then from a scholar here and there (for those who care, his tale is really quite dreadful on so many levels), but he himself gets relatively little coverage when compared to the Clerk and Miller (whose tales feature adolescents and emerging adults caught in the throes of lustful desires—plus two crabby old men); the Wife of Bath (whose tale features a young bachelor, twenty-four dancing maidens—plus a hideous old hag); and his own father, the Knight (whose tale features a teenage love triangle of two young knights trying to outcompete one another for a young maiden forced to pick between the two—plus some old folks).

The storytelling Squire—bless his adolescent emerging adult soul—is the one who blew this whole history-of-adolescence thing wide open for me. He broke all the rules of established historiography. If way back in the fourteenth century, a twenty-year-old squire's appearance, actions, attitudes, personal interactions, societal limitations, and cultural roles were described in ways that echo contemporary descriptions of adolescents on one hand and emerging adults on the other, what other things might people have been saying and singing and painting and thinking in regards to fourteen- to twenty-something-year-olds throughout history?

I asked myself: Was the Squire just an anomaly? A singular fluke of literary genius?

After years of reading and research, I answered my own question: No. He wasn't. (An anomaly or a fluke, that is.)

It turns out that Chaucer was not the only pre-1900 guy with specific views about those who were past childhood but not yet at full adulthood. Nor were his views different from others in the degree to which they resemble modern depictions and understanding.

It also turns out that historians have been researching, discussing, and writing about "adolescence throughout history" for the past forty years or so. When my search for historical adolescence led me to the historians, and when I started to read them in earnest, I was surprised. What they were saying flew in the face of the comfortable narrative so many of us accept.[22]

When I started to read the source material itself—including medical texts, court records, poetry, ballads, stories, autobiographies, conduct manuals, parenting guides, news items, dictionaries, and sermons—I was convinced. For most of history, with some variations here and there as societies went through significant changes or upheaval, there was a very clear understanding of a stage of life that followed childhood and preceded adulthood. The in-between that we call adolescence is a longstanding reality. Certainly the experiences of adolescents have shifted and altered throughout the years, sometimes significantly, but the concept has always existed in some shape or another.

BEFORE WE BEGIN OUR SEARCH …

As often happens when people have differing viewpoints or interpretations of a particular subject, the discussions currently centered around adolescence—especially in terms of its "invention" or discovery—are at least partly shaped by the definitions we attach to the word itself.

When we say *adolescence*, do we mean nothing more than the years of a person's life between ages fourteen and twenty-something? Or do we mean certain biological changes that occur during that specific span of years? Or do we mean specific attitudes and behaviors that often manifest themselves during that specific span of years? Or do we mean the cultural constraints that are placed on people of that specific age group?

Or do we mean the unique institutions that enclose and cater to those people? Or do we mean the psycho-social moratorium that currently defines the teenage years?

Yes. People do mean those things. All of them, in different combinations and to different degrees.

If someone says "adolescence is new" and means by that "*the practice of sequestering American teenagers in high school for four years* is new," then that person is correct. But if someone says "adolescence is new" and by that means "*the stage of life following childhood when a person has developed sexually but is neither viewed nor functions as a full adult in society* is new," then that person is wrong.

Our understanding and use of the word *adolescent* is affected by whatever conversational frame we inhabit, including biology, developmental psychology, anthropology, and sociology. Since this book is written primarily for youth workers, I'll use the term **adolescence** to indicate **the stage of life that includes the latter part of middle school, all of high school, and an unspecified amount of college**. Or: the stage of life extending from age thirteen (give or take a year) through the legal voting age of eighteen (or the legal drinking age of twenty-one, or later). Or: the stage of life extending from puberty up to the time when a person assumes all the roles and responsibilities of adulthood (whenever that is and whatever those may be).

> SIMPLY PUT: Adolescence is the stage of life following childhood and preceding adulthood, when a person is not still a child but not yet an adult.

For adolescents themselves, this stage of life simply *is*. They get up each day, do and think and feel all sorts of things, go to bed at night, and probably never once think to themselves, "I'm an adolescent." They may think, "I'm sick of being treated like a kid," or, "When I'm an adult, I'll never be like that," wherein *that* often refers to the behavior of a parent, teacher, or other authority figure toward them or others.

For adults, this stage of life is often viewed in terms of expectations, worries, fears, and hopes, both for now and the future. Those expectations, worries, fears, and hopes— regardless of how realistic, justified, irrational, or neurotic they may be—are a legacy that stretches throughout history. While our culture has changed wildly, far beyond the death of the card catalog, our ideas and attitudes about adolescence have remained surprisingly consistent. Whether that is good, bad, or something else entirely remains to be seen.

Either way, this book is intended primarily to help start a conversation that extends beyond the current narrative about the short history of adolescence.

WHAT THIS BOOK IS NOT:

1. An exhaustive analysis of all the pertinent source material throughout history. It simply isn't possible to offer anything more than glimpses of various historical evidence and realities that will hopefully begin to fill in the current pre-1900 looming gap. For those who are interested, the Additional Sources on page 137 provides a more extensive (but far from exhaustive) list of further reading.

2. An attempt to define (or redefine) the term *adolescence* for every writer, scholar, and youth worker, or an attempt to put parameters on how the word is used. Rather, this is a first step in remapping the historical narrative of adolescence with the full realization that some people—because of their particular use or understanding of the term—will not find the historical threads interesting or significant.

3. A final word on the matter. Final words, unless from the mouth of God, are generally ill-advised. This book rather offers a new look at an old idea (the recent social construct of adolescence) by way of even older ideas (historical documents) that will hopefully give all of us some new things to consider as we continue to learn about, spend time with, and minister to adolescents.

4. A new practical handbook for how youth ministry programming should change in light of this new historical vantage point. Dodgeball will still be a popular choice for some and a frightening proposition for others. Food games are still going to make a mess. Church vans are still going to cause a plaguey fuss. Camp trips are still going to require fundraising. I hope you will read this book even so.

WHAT THIS BOOK IS:

1. A sliver of historical evidence that places us on a very long continuum of adults with distinct views and opinions about adolescence.

2. An attempt to jumpstart a new conversation, one that considers youth ministry in light of a longer historical context.

3. A first step towards reorienting youth ministry on a more accurate cultural map.

4. A consideration of the possible "so what" implications of the historical record regarding adolescence.

Let the search begin.

ENDNOTES

1. Matt Walsh, "Adolescence: A Modern Plague, But There Is a Cure," The Matt Walsh Blog, September 2013, https://themattwalshblog.wordpress. com/2013/09/28/adolescence-a-modern-plague-but-there-is-a-cure/.
2. Joseph F. Kett, "Discovery and Invention," *Journal of Adolescent Health* 14:8 (December 1993), 605.
3. Kenneth J. Saltman, "The Social Construction of Adolescence," *The Critical Middle School Reader*, eds. Enora R. Brown and Kenneth J. Saltman (New York: Routledge, 2005), 15-20.
4. Kenneth Keniston, *Youth and Dissent: The Rise of a New Opposition* (New York: Harcourt Brace Jovanovich, 1971), 4.
5. James E. Côté and Anton L. Allahar, *Generation on Hold: Coming of Age in the Late Twentieth Century* (New York: New York University Press, 1996).
6. Lisa Wade PhD, "The Invention of 'Adolescence,' " The Society Pages (blog), February 2011, http://thesocietypages.org/ socimages/2011/02/23/the-invention-of-adolescence/.
7. From page viii in the preface to *Adolescent Medicine: A Handbook for Primary Care* (Lippincott Williams and Wilkins, 2006).
8. Apprenticeships, puberty, and other adolescent realities will be discussed throughout the coming chapters. Information on the signers of the Declaration of Independence can be found at http://www. archives.gov/exhibits/charters/declaration_signers_gallery_facts.pdf.
9. Robert Epstein, in a 2007 interview with Hara Estroff Marano, "Trashing Teens," *Psychology Today* (March 2007). The article was peer-reviewed again in 2012, suggesting that its authority still stands.
10. Philippe Ariès, *Centuries of Childhood: A Social History of Family Life*, trans. Robert Baldick (New York: Vintage, 1962), 128. Originally published in French as *L'Enfant et la Vie Familiale sous l'Ancien Regime* (Paris: Librairie Plon, 1960), 30.
11. One of these is the historian Barbara Hanawalt, a leading expert on historical childhood and adolescence, who notes that Ariès' "startling conclusions [are] problematic because of his careless use of historical evidence" (22). "The Child in the Middle Ages and the Renaissance," *Beyond the Century of the Child*, eds. William Koops and Michael Zuckerman (Philadelphia: University of Pennsylvania Press, 2003), 21-42.
12. Two recent exceptions are Theresa O'Keefe (Boston College) whose 2010 paper "Growing Up Alone: the new normal of isolation in adolescence" (http://www.aymeducators.org/wp-content/uploads/ Growing-up-Alone-Isolation-in-Adolescence-by-Theresa-OKeefe.pdf)

considers the possible implications of Barbara Hanawalt and David Herlihy's historical research when applied to Chap Clark's theories and conclusions in his book *Hurt*; and Mark Senter (Emeritus, Trinity Evangelical Divinity School) whose book *When God Shows Up: A History of Protestant Youth Ministry in America* (Baker Academic, 2010) considers the roots of American-based youth ministry back to the early 1800s.

13. Conducted by Adam McLane: "The Adolescence Survey," The Youth Cartel, August 26, 2014 - September 25, 2014 (online survey).

14. These numbers can be found in various sources, including The National Bureau of Economic Research: Michael R. Haines, "Long Term Marriage Patterns in the United States from Colonial Times to the Present," March 1996, nber.org; Edwin J. Perkins, *The Economy of Colonial America* second edition (New York: Columbia University Press, 1988); et al.

15. Hildegard of Bingen, *Causae et Curae*, discussed in many contemporary overviews of medieval medicine including Joan Cadden, *The Meanings of Sex Differences in the Middle Ages* (Cambridge: Cambridge University Press, 1993), 86.

16. These general ages of puberty—twelve for girls and fourteen for boys— appear in numerous medieval texts. See, for example: Luke Demaitre, "The Idea of Childhood and Child Care in Medical Writings of the Middle Ages," *The Journal of Psychohistory* 4 (1977), 461-490.

17. Historical data on apprenticeships is extensive, including: Kathryn L. Reyerson, "The Adolescent Apprentice/Worker in Medieval Montpellier," *Journal of Family History* 17:4 (1992), 353-370; Barbara Hanawalt, *Growing Up in Medieval London* (New York: Oxford University Press, 1993); Barbara A. Hanawalt and David J. Wallace, eds., " 'The Childe of Bristowe' and the Making of Middle-Class Adolescence," *Bodies and Disciplines: Intersections of Literature and History in Fifteenth-Century England* (Minneapolis: University of Minnesota Press, 1996), 155-178; Alan MacFarlane, ed., *The Diary of Ralph Josselin 1616-1683* (London: Oxford University Press, 1976); et al.

18. "*adolescence*, n." OED Online. January 2015. Oxford University Press. http://www.oed.com.ezproxy.lib.purdue.edu/view/Entry/2648?redirectedFrom=adolescence (accessed January 2015). "*family*, n. and adj." OED Online. January 2015. Oxford University Press. http://www.oed.com.ezproxy.lib.purdue.edu/view/Entry/67975?redirectedFrom=family (accessed January 2015).

19. The Google Ngram Viewer charts the frequency of words or phrases in printed sources within the scanned corpus. For more details see: https://books.google.com/ngrams/info.

20. I ran the Ngram Viewer through the general "English" corpus. Switching to "American English," "British English," or "English One Million" complicates the findings even more.

21. G. Stanley Hall, *Adolescence: Its Psychology and Its Relations to Physiology, Anthropology, Sociology, Sex, Crime, Religion, and Education* (New York: D. Appleton and Company, 1904).

22. The list of historians is long: Barbara Hanawalt (The Ohio State University, Emeritus), Nicholas Orme (University of Exeter), Jeremy Goldberg (University of York), Rudolph Bell (Rutgers), Albrecht Classen (University of Arizona), Sally Crawford (University of Oxford, archeology), Natalie Zemon Davis (University of Toronto), David Herlihy (Brown University, d. 1991), Kim Phillips (University of Aukland), Shulamith Shahar (Tel Aviv University, ret.), Ilana Krausman Ben-Amos (Ben-Gurion University), Deborah Youngs (Swansea University), and others.

THE THINKERS II

Thinkers think. Doers do. And rarely the twain do meet. Or so goes the popular commentary about Thinkers and Doers, especially in reference to some vaguely ethereal world of ivory-tower academics on the one hand and a more concrete and pragmatically programmed world of in-the-trenches practitioners on the other.

Both metaphors—towers and trenches—are pitifully reductionist, as though the life of academia is nothing but an enchanted fairytale and the life of a practitioner nothing but one long bloody battle.

Thinkers engage in substantive *doing* of all kinds of things just as Doers engage in substantive *thinking* about all manner of topics. Perhaps nowhere should Thinkers and Doers be more closely aligned and vitally connected than in youth ministry where research and theories inform ministry practices that then inform the lives of real teenagers. Those who shape the field with their research and thinking must certainly be involved in the lives of young people at some level in order to focus on the thinking that matters. Those who minister to teenagers must be continually thinking about why they do what they do and how new findings and studies might have an effect on their daily ministry. The stakes are high. There is no room for empty theorizing or uninformed practice.

In other words, today's youth ministry Thinkers and Doers should be grateful for one another and should pay attention to each other.

They should also listen carefully both to other Thinkers (in different academic fields and various social contexts) and other Doers (in different ministries and various social institutions). Cross-discipline, cross-ministerial, and cross-cultural conversations are much too rare; that rarity is one reason, perhaps, for the staying power of the adolescence-is-new narrative that undergirds many youth ministry conversations. We have ignored the historians—or at least been unaware of them—and in the process missed out on opportunities to engage with a longer and wider sampling of knowledge and experiences.

Additionally, we have been guilty—like so many other moderns and postmoderns—of believing we know much more than previous generations not just of our own era but every other era. We are ironically both Whiggishly exultant—"Look how much we know about adolescence and everything else!"—and despondently morose—"Things have never been worse for adolescents and everyone else!" We like to own both extremes and embody both realities.

It's a human tendency that appears throughout history, this need to be both better informed and worse off than those who went before us.

Those of us in the twenty-first century certainly have more access to more information about more things than at any other time in history. But that does not necessarily mean we are smarter or know more. The twentieth century did not give birth to thinking, and long before we had calculators and computers and smartphones and Google to spoon-feed us gargantuan amounts of facts and data, we had brains that were busy with such tangly topics as calculus, astronomy, philosophy, and human biology. Lucky for us, the devices of yesteryear still work and the premodern operating systems still compute. Score ten points for vellum, the Roman alphabet, and basic grammar—all of which are still fully functional a thousand years later. We would do well to not ignore them any longer because there was much significant thinking going on long before any of us showed up.

INFORMATION SYSTEMS AND THE CONVERSATION

Before computer operating systems, systematic theology, Wikipedia, Google analytics, and peer-reviewed journals, Thinkers were hard at work, sorting, cataloging, and codifying information. The proverbial systems guy has a long and storied past.[1] He has been around for as long as humanity has existed, and he has created systems and codes for wide-ranging topics such as rhetoric, war, law, morality, business, even love, as well as for the necessary storage of such topics by means of language, syntax, scribing, and printing. The smallest detail of the broadest topic had a proper function, application, and place that was then recorded with the proper signs, symbols, and notations.

Perhaps the most familiar and most visible information system throughout history has been that of human life—dividing humanity into its various ages and sub-ages (e.g., infancy, childhood, youth, adulthood, etc.).[2] We see it in ancient writings, and we continue to use it today in almost every context: schools, churches, families, consumer markets, entertainment industries, and civic laws. As populations grow and programs expand, those distinct age classifications continue to be refined and narrowed, a tendency that is as old as that of dividing the human life into distinct stages.

In the fourteenth century, the third dialogue in Petrarch's *Secretum* includes these lines spoken by Augustine:

> Some divide even the shortest life into four parts, some into six, some into even more parts. That's how you try to extend the smallest of things; not by increasing its length, which cannot be done, but by dividing its parts. But what's the point of all this subdividing? Invent as many little parts as you please; they are gone in a moment, in the twinkling of an eye.[3]

He was commenting on how adults, especially as they grow older, sometimes look back on life and identify more and more different stages. Maybe it's an attempt to slow the aging process. Maybe it's an attempt to claim their exclusive position of authority. We still do that, don't we? As children, we assume "the kids' table" is a firmly established institution, created perhaps on the day of Cain's birth. It simply *is*, and there is no use fussing about it. As adults we know better. The kids' table is one of the few domains over which we reign in full splendor and glory. Please: Let's not have any intergenerational rubbing of the shoulders when there are mashed potatoes and seven kinds of pie at stake.

In our churches, where Rubbing of the Intergenerational Shoulders should be as sacred as the passing of the peace, we sometimes get very caught up in (and carried away with) creating as many non-shoulder rubbing contexts as possible, not just between the generations but within them as well. Church nurseries are divided into infants, crawlers, and walkers. Elementary students are divided into K-2, pre-tweens, and tweens. Adolescents are divided into early adolescents, adolescents, late adolescents, and extended adolescents. Adults are divided into young adults, emerging adults, adult adults, middle-aged adults, retired adults, and senior adults. Within these are additional vocational and familial subcategories: young professionals, young singles, single professionals, young marrieds, young families, empty-nesters, semi-retireds, and various other combinations.

We love our groups, subgroups, and sub-subgroups. They give us a sense of identity, a place to belong, and a scaffolding in which to exist. The smaller the subgroup, the more distinctly unique and more narrowly targeted. Of course, such subdivisions are more than just an existential attempt at slowing down life, as Petrarch wrote. Identifying smaller cohesive units does serve a practical purpose as it helps us articulate desired learning outcomes, identify best pedagogical strategies, and even choose appropriate snacks, all with an eye towards successful ministry. Depending on the age group, we might triangulate the following things:

> God's love + motion songs + goldfish
> Jesus' redemptive work + dodgeball + pizza
> new-Calvinist spiritual practices + streaming video +
>   ethnically diverse meals
> end-times symbolism + typed study guide + coffee cake

Age divisions provide a simple identifying label that is rarely self-invoked during the first few decades of life. I have never heard a toddler, tween, adolescent, or emerging adult identify themselves as such, though I have heard them refer to other people by a specific age label.

Regarding adolescence (it) and adolescents (them)—which we'll call *adolescentce* when referring to both *it* and *them* collectively—it is adults who exclusively categorize, label, identify, and describe. They have been doing it for a very, very long time, even before adolescence was "discovered" and "invented" in the late 1800s. What follows is a summary blitz of various ways certain Thinkers—philosophers, astronomers, doctors, and etymologists—have been defining and describing adolescence for the past 1000-plus years.

CODIFYING LIFE: THE AGES OF MAN

Depending on one's area of specialty (biology, physiology, astronomy, theology, pedagogy, artistry, poetry) and one's point of reference (the seasons, the bodily humors, the elements, the months, the planets), the number of distinct life stages were believed to range from three to twelve. Regardless of how many stages were identified, every Ages of Man system, as they were called, included an age that bridged childhood and adulthood— sometimes called simply "youth" but many times called more specifically "adolescence."

In general, all the different theories agreed that adolescence began with puberty. Numerous medical treatises from 1250 to 1500 were concerned with specific issues of childhood, lasting up to age twelve or fourteen depending on one's sex. At that age, puberty began and the child was ushered into adolescence. As mentioned in Chapter One, some writers observed that in certain cases, children were reaching puberty before the expected age of twelve for girls and fourteen for boys and in at least one instance suggested this was due to better nutrition. Or perhaps "gluttony," as you may recall.

Much like today, there was less agreement about when adolescence ended. Some said eighteen, others said twenty-one, still others said twenty-four. At least a few Thinkers put that number even later. It may not have been termed "extended adolescence" or "emerging adulthood" but it was described in similar ways, with deep-seated concerns about those who failed to settle on a respectable trade or avoided settling down to established adult roles and responsibilities.

Beyond defining adolescence by just biological age and physical growth, most Thinkers included a list of expected behaviors and attitudes. In other words, adolescence wasn't just about being fourteen or sixteen or eighteen. It was also a stage of identity formation that included a person's thoughts, emotions, actions, and spiritual understanding. Today, we know that many of the defining characteristics of adolescence are due to a changing brain and body. Back then, Thinkers assumed that such changes were a result of planetary influence, shifts in the balance of bodily humors (blood, bile, phlegm), seasonal changes, the natural elements, or any combination thereof. Importantly, all of the premodern Ages of Man schemes were related to things in the natural realm because the various ages were considered to be *naturally occurring*—not culturally constructed—though certainly many of the outer trappings (fashion, for example) were shaped and influenced by culture.

The end of adolescence, at whatever age it may occur, was the start of complete independence and full adulthood.

In many ways, these early theories were the precursors to the grand theories of the twentieth century put forth by Erik Erikson, Jean Piaget, Sigmund Freud, and others. They codified life stages in terms of biological growth, intellectual capabilities, behavioral tendencies, and spiritual understanding.

In the fourth century BC, Aristotle provided one of the first lengthy descriptions of the age he called youth, which included both what we today would call adolescence and young adulthood. He did not use the word *adolescence* (which is of Latin origin, and he wrote in Greek), but there is no doubt this is the stage he was referring to. In his theory about how best to influence, persuade, understand, empathize, and communicate with people of various ages, he includes startlingly familiar descriptions of those who are old enough to reason—i.e., those past childhood. He divides these people into three groups: youth, manhood, and old age.

He describes youth as those who ...

> are always eager and ready to carry out their desires;
> have strong sensual passions;
> lack the discipline and self-control to rein in their sensual desires (read: can't say no);
> are changeable and fickle in their desires;
> are naturally hot-tempered and impulsive;
> hate being slighted or mocked;
> want to be admired, but want to win even more;
> are naturally hot-blooded;
> hope and expect to do great things;
> are extremely fond of their friends and want to be with them as much as possible;
> often do things to excess—loving, hating, and everything else;
> think they know everything.[4]

A few centuries later, Claudius Ptolemy (mathematician, astronomer, geographer, and master of other smart-guy Thinker pursuits) offered a more elaborate and detailed age system that included seven distinct stages, each directly influenced by a specific planet.[5]

He said that the moon controls infants and children up to age four—presumably because they behave like lunatics now and then.

Mercury, he said, controls children from age four through thirteen: learning starts in earnest, the soul's intellect and logic begin to develop, individual characteristics begin to appear, and physical activity increases.

He said that youth—ages fourteen through twenty-one— belongs exclusively to Venus, the goddess of love.

> Venus, taking in charge the third age, that of youth, for the next eight years, corresponding in number to her own period, begins, *as is natural*, to inspire, at their maturity, an activity of the seminal passages and to implant an impulse toward the embrace of love. At this time particularly a kind of frenzy enters the soul— incontinence, desire for any chance sexual gratification, burning passion, guile, and the blindness of the impetuous lover.[6] (emphasis mine)

Yes, let's pause.

Seminal passages, frenzied incontinence, sexual gratification, and impetuously burning passion—all in a single paragraph. Ought we to giggle at the ridiculousness of it? Snort at the outrageousness of it? Rally against the stereotypicalness of it? Or—in equally stereotypical fashion—welcome Ptolemy to the world of middle school youth ministry insider jokes? (I generalize. Overly.)

Perhaps the most common and popular theory of life stages came from Isidore of Seville (d. 636 AD) who described six distinct ages: infancy, childhood, adolescence, youth, maturity, and old age. Adolescence, he said, is "mature enough for

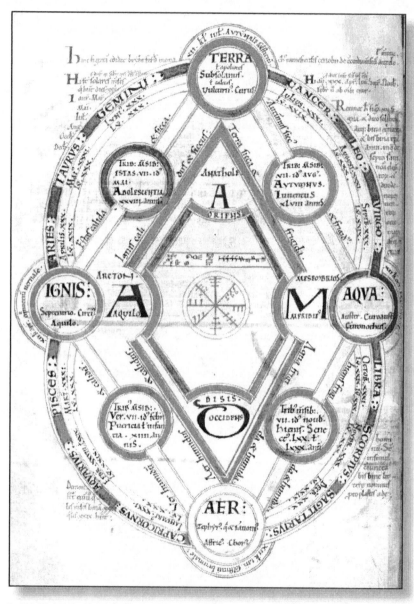

Byrhtferth's "Diagram of the Physical and Physiological Fours." Reproduced by permission of the President and Fellows of St. John's College, Oxford. Manuscript 17, folio 7v. Image can be found online at: http://bit.ly/1Kjo9ee.

procreating and lasts until the twenty-eighth year."[7] Youth, historically a more malleable term than adolescence, was for Isidore a description of the first years of full maturity that started in a person's late twenties. As time went on, youth became more closely aligned with adolescence specifically.

One century later, the Venerable Bede wrote about four distinct stages of life: childhood, youth, maturity, and old age. His childhood roughly equated to Isidore's infancy and childhood; his youth roughly equated to Isidore's adolescence; his maturity roughly equated to Isidore's youth and maturity. In the late tenth century, the English monk Byrhtferth used a system much like Bede's to create an early infographic that was reproduced in numerous manuscripts and books. He designed four quadrants of data about the seasons, the elements, the months, the bodily humors, the constellations, and the four corresponding ages of man.[8] In the bottom left quadrant of the image shown is *infantia* and *pueritia* lasting until age fourteen. In the top left is *adolescentia*, lasting until age twenty-eight. The top right is *juventus*, lasting until age forty-eight. Bottom right is *senectus*, lasting until age seventy. Or eighty. Or presumably for as long as a person was still breathing.

While Byrhtferth's diagram does not specify what the adolescent experience was like in the early Middle Ages, it clearly indicates that adolescence was a recognized and described stage of life that occurred *after* childhood and *before* adulthood. Many scholarly manuscripts from that era were written exclusively in Latin, read by only the most learned. But Byrhtferth was not exclusive. He immediately followed the Latin of this section on the different ages with a translation into the vernacular Old English, "so that what is clearly understood by monks may also be known to clerics"[9]—monks being the primary communicators to Thinkers and clerics being the primary communicator to Doers. This knowledge, then, wasn't just for elite intellectuals.

MORE THEORIES ON THE AGES OF MAN

About the same time, Ælfric, Abbot of Eynsham, related a
similar view of human development, though his was based
on the day's hours and included five, rather than four, stages.
Rather than Latin—the learned language of the day—this Ages
of Man theory is written exclusively in the vernacular. Ælfric
says that childhood is like morning; adolescence is like the
third hour, "on which rises our youth, just as the sun does at
about the third hour"; completed growth is like midday; old
age is the ninth hour; and very old age is the eleventh hour.
His theory paralleled one put forward by Pope Gregory, with
one major change: where Gregory listed *adolescentia* and
juventus (adolescence and young adulthood) as two separate
stages, Ælfric combines these into a single stage of life, a kind
of adolescence-plus-emerging-adulthood season that together
bridged childhood and full adulthood.[10]

John Trevisa's English translation of Bartholomaeus Anglicus'
The Properties of Things (*De Proprietatibum Rerum*) was wildly
popular in its day. In this scheme, adolescence was said to start
at fourteen (following infancy, childhood, and boyhood) and
last until twenty-one, or in some cases twenty-eight, and in rare
cases, even thirty. May, the month when "all things that are alive
are moved to joy and love," was associated with this age group.
Like others, Trevisa didn't believe there was a specific age when
full adulthood arrived. Reasoning started in adolescence, and
so they could be expected to learn and do more. But even so,
he said, they still required the oversight of a recognized adult to
adhere to rules and structure, sometimes even after adolescence
was done.[11]

These various theories about the different Ages of Man tended to be equitable; they described and discussed each stage in equal measure. But in at least a few instances, adolescence was not simply one age among many but rather its own topic of study and discussion.

A stunning example of this is found in an oversized (twelve inches by eighteen inches) late fourteenth-century book called *Omne Bonum*, or *All Good Things*, the first alphabetically arranged encyclopedia of information covering a wide base of knowledge and topics.[12] Included among such important *A* entries as *Abraham*, *Advocatus* (lawyer), *Adventus* (advent), *Alimenta* (food), *Allegoricus* (allegory), *Amor* (love), *Amicicia* (friendship), *Angeli* (angels), *Anima* (soul), *Anglia* (England), *Apocrifum* (Apocrypha), *Aqua* (water), *Aquila* (eagle), *Abores* (trees), *Aves* (birds), and *Aurora* (dawn), is a full page-and-a-half entry for *Adolescens*.[13]

Yep, *that* adolescence. The one that includes people who are no longer children but neither fully adults (at least not in the opinion of those who are further along the fully adult journey).

The entry—one of the longer ones—includes information on the legal status of adolescents, some observations on Matthew 19:16-22, discussion about several different Ages of Man schemes, and a passage from a well-known commentary that says adolescents are prone to evil and are in need of firm control. "It is better to restrain hot youths so that those given over to cupidity may not make a sad end."[14]

Perhaps even more interesting than the text is the bright historiated initial *A* that opens the entry and is pictured on the cover of this book. If pictures aim to speak a thousand words, this one succeeds. (More about that in Chapter Three: The Creators.)

These life stage systems continued to be known and referenced long after they first appeared, with little variation. Still in 1668, a person could easily find the common outline of infancy → childhood → adolescency → youth → manhood → declining age.[15] It would be fair to say that for more than a thousand years, people clung as tightly to the different Ages of Man narratives as we do to the Adolescence Is New narrative. Our tenacious tendencies haven't changed much.

Admittedly, there is no way to know how many people in previous centuries were intimately familiar with the Ages of Man systems, any more than we can know how many people today are intimately familiar with the most recent human development theories. Nor can we know how many people in previous centuries knew what the philosophers and astronomers said about the stage called adolescence.

"The Seven Ages of Man" from Charles Hoole, *Orbis Sensualium Pictus. Joh. Amos Commenius' Visible World, or, A Picture and Nomenclature of all the chief Things that are in the World, and of Mens Employments therein. For the use of Young Latine-Scholars* (London: Printed for J. Kirton, at the Kings-Arms, in Saint Paules Churchyard, 1659). Image published with permission of ProQuest. Further reproduction is prohibited without permission. Image produced by ProQuest as part of *Early English Books Online*. www.proquest.com

This Latin textbook for children was reprinted by Encyclopedia Britannica in 1887, where it was described as "an educational classic of prime importance," "the first picture book ever made for children," and "for a century the most popular textbook in England" (iii, Editor's Preface). The original version was translated into many European languages. This English translation, shown here, was published in numerous editions from 1659 through 1777 and was printed in both England and America. Note that Youth (*adolescens*) is between Boy and Young-man; Damosel (*puella*) is between Girle and Maid. Based on printing history and educational tracts from the seventeeth through the nineteenth century, the popularity and widespread use of this book suggest that many children (and parents and teachers) were familiar with this theory of human development. While this presentation of the seven ages does not provide details on behaviors, attitudes, and social realities, it is strong evidence for the general understanding of a distinct life stage between childhood and adulthood.

(76)

XXXVII.

Septem Ætates Hominis.

The Seven Ages of Man.

(77)

A Man is
first an Infant, 1.
then a Boy, 2.
then a Youth, 3.
then a Young-man, 4.
then a Man, 5.
after that, an Elderly-
and at last, (man, 6.
a decrepid old Man, 7.

So also
in the other fex,
there are, a Girle, 8.
a Damofel, 9.
a Maid, 10.
a Woman, 11.
an Elderly Woman,12.
and a decrepid old
Woman. 13.

Homo eſt
primùm *Infans*, 1.
deinde *Puer*, 2.
tum *Adoleſcens*, 3.
inde *Juvenis*, 4.
pofteà *Vir*, 5.
dehinc *Senex*, 6.
tandem
Silicernium. 7.

Sic etiam
in altero Sexu,
funt, *Pupa*, 8.
Puella, 9.
Virgo, 10.
Mulier, 11.
Vetula, 12.

Anus decrepita. 13.

Certainly if the term and the accompanying descriptions showed up only in what might be viewed as academic texts, it might be fair to speculate—cautiously—that the general populace had absolutely no idea people passed through various developmental stages, and therefore had no idea that roles and responsibilities and behaviors and expectations might vary with different ages, and therefore assumed that everyone abruptly moved from childhood to adulthood with no transitional in-between stage.

But the technical term *adolescence* and the more common term *youth*, and their standard definitions and descriptions show up in many other documents and social contexts, including the most basic of all: the dictionary.

WEBSTER'S PREDECESSORS

As noted earlier, it's dangerous to assert that a social/cultural entity did or did not exist based entirely on word evidence, especially if the assertion is negative. "X did not exist in the past because the word X didn't exist and wasn't used back then" is a difficult argument to defend. Equally difficult would be "X was a word back then and it was used with some regularity and so everyone back then must have known everything there was to know about X and everyone must have personally experienced X in the same way and to the same degree."

Both of those are nonsense.

But if "X" shows up in a variety of sources, then certainly at least some people knew about it, even if it was just the specific authors and readers.

Dictionaries—while not most people's first choice for leisure reading—were at one time the most basic collection of data for the most lay-level scholar. If adolescence hadn't been invented and didn't exist prior to the late 1800s, then certainly a person shouldn't be able to find any dictionary entries for it before that time. But in my search for adolescence, I found specific entries in over forty distinct dictionaries ranging from 1538 to the late 1700s.[16] A handful of those are foreign language dictionaries because apparently it was important—even in the pocket editions—to know the correct word for *adolescence* in French, Italian, Portuguese, Latin, Persian, Arabic, Gaellic, and Welsh.

[By the way, English has changed significantly over the centuries, especially in terms of spelling, in part because pronunciation has changed but also because phonics tended to rule the day. Reclaiming the kindergarten reading strategy of *sounding it out* will help navigate the archaic spellings that follow here and in later chapters.]

The first printed dictionary, compiled by Sir Thomas Elliot, appeared in 1538 and includes the following:

> **Adolescentia** *is the aege betwene chyldehode and mannes age, which is betwene xiiii and xxi.*

> **Adolescentior:** *to be wanton, or full of youthe*

A New World of English Words, or a General Dictionary (1658) defines *adolescence* as the age of youth, *puberty* as the start of youth, and *adult* as full ripeness of age.

A Physical Dictionary: In Which, All the Terms Relating Either to Anatomy, Chirurgery [Surgery]*, Pharmacy, or Chymstry Are Very Accurately Explain'd* (1684) says that bodies go through significant changes due to "the continual action and fermentation of the blood and spirits" (i.e., it is natural to develop and behave in certain ways at certain ages); of the six distinct ages, *adolescence* is said to last until eighteen, *youth* until twenty-five.

The *Universal Etymological Dictionary* of 1721 defines *adolescence* as "the flower of youth; the state from fourteen to twenty-five or thirty in men, and from twelve to twenty-one in women."

The age span was often adjusted slightly for males and females in this way. This dictionary indicates that the average age of puberty is fourteen for boys and twelve for girls.

A dictionary compiled especially for females, *The Ladies Dictionary, Being a General Entertainment of the Fair-Sex, A Work Never Attempted Before in English* (1694) highlighted these age differences even more specifically. For men, fourteen marked the age of discretion and twenty-one marked the age of adulthood. Women were discrete enough at eleven to consent to a betrothal, but were only capable of confirming that consent at twenty-one. *Youthhood or Adolescence* "consists of eight years, that from fourteen to two and twenty."

A Compleat [sic] English Dictionary Containing the True Meaning of all Words in the English Language (1735) includes the very brief entry: *adolescence*: the flower of youth.

In 1737 the revised version was titled:

> *A New English Dictionary Containing a Large and Almost Compleat Collection of Useful English Words. Those of NO Real Use, with Which the Larger Works of This Sort Are Generally Stuff'd, Being Entirely Omitted.*

Adolescence is included, just as it is in the 1741 revision titled:

> *A New Dictionary of All Such English Words (with Their Explanations) As Are Generally Made Use of, in Speaking or Writing the English Language*

A *Dictionary of Art and Sciences* (1754) says that adolescence lasts from twelve to twenty-five for boys and from twelve to twenty-one for girls.

The New Royal English Dictionary (1780) says that childhood is the "interval between infancy and youth" and *adolescency* (an equivalent word that was often used) is the "state between puberty and manhood."

At least a few dictionaries include even more specific details about not only when adolescence occurs but also what it looks like.

1770 saw the printing of *The Universal Spelling Book: Or a New and Easy Guide to the English Language (for Schools) Includes Many Useful Things Necessary to Help the Young Beginner and Inform the More Grown-Up Youth, with Chronological Tables of the Monarchs and Kings of England, and Other Most Remarkable Occurrences in Sacred and Prophane History; With Some Short Remarks Upon the Seven Stages of Life, Which Are Not Only Improving to the Mind and Morals; But May Be of Great Service to Prevent Youth from Falling a Sacrifice to the Common Temptations of Life and Their Own Unguarded Passions.* (Pause here to breathe, please. They sure knew how to title a book back then.)

Adolescence is here defined simply as "youthfulness." But in a discussion of the seven stages of life, the author writes this about adolescence to the adolescent reader:

> We are now apt to think ourselves much happier in this stage than the last, because at fifteen or sixteen years, youth think they are capable of taking the reins in their own hands, and guiding themselves ... Watch therefore and be sober. Forsake not the advice of thy parents and friends, which will arm thee against temptations, and thou wilt certainly be happy: but if thou refuseth instruction, thou wilt be led captive to thy shame and sorrow ...

Though adolescents were encouraged to heed the advice of parents, it was also understood that they now preferred to do most of their own thinking. Emanuel Swedenborg's *New Dictionary of Correspondences* (1794) says that adolescence is "the state when man begins to think and act for himself, and not from the instruction or direction of others."

At the same time, even as they were doing more and more of their own thinking, there were still opinions about how efficient, intelligent, and wise that thinking was, or perhaps was not. That might be why the author M. William Birnie, when dedicating a rather advanced book to the seventeen-year-old James Hamilton, Marquess, included this statement about the young man's advanced ability to fully understand the text:

> Your minde, thogh yet adolescent, is so magnifickly inner-manned.

What could be better than having a "magnifickly inner-manned" mind? It sounds so entirely grown-up. Or dull, depending on one's view, much like theories, definitions, and dictionary entries. Mere words may prove a point—that *adolescence* was recognized as a stage of life between childhood and adulthood; but they don't do much to enliven and engage the imagination.

For that, we turn to the Creators.

ENDNOTES

1. C. S. Lewis, *The Discarded Image* (Cambridge: Cambridge University Press, 1964), 10. "At his most characteristic, medieval man was not a dreamer nor a wanderer. He was an organiser, a codifier, a builder of systems ... [d]istinction, definition, tabulation were his delight ... [of] all our modern inventions I suspect that they would most have admired the card index."

2. J. A. Burrow, *The Ages of Man: A Study in Medieval Writing and Thought* (Oxford: Clarendon Press, 1988); Elizabeth Sears, *The Ages of Man: Medieval Interpretations of the Life Cycle* (Princeton: Princeton University Press, 1986); et al.

3. In Petrarch's original Latin, this reads: "*[A]ngustissimam etatem alii in quattuor, alli in sex particulas, aliique in plures etiam distribuunt; ita rem minimam, quia quantitate non licet, numero tentatis extendere. Quid autem sectio ista confert? Finge quotlibet particulas; omnes in ictu oculi prope simul evanescunt.*"

4. See Aristotle, *Art of Rhetoric*, trans. J. H. Freese, Loeb Classical Library 193 (1926; repr. Cambridge, MA: Harvard University Press, 2006), Book II, Chapter 12 (14-151).

5. The ancient and medieval world identified seven planets: Moon, Mercury, Venus, Sun, Mars, Jupiter, and Saturn.

6. Ptolemy, *Tetrabiblios*, ed. and trans. F. E. Robbins (Cambridge, MA: Harvard University Press, 1940), IV. 10 (443-44).

7. Isidor of Seville, *The Etymologic of Isidore of Seville*, trans. Stephen A. Barney, et al. (Cambridge University Press, [1926] 2006), IL. ii. 1-4 (241).

8. Byrhtferth, *Byrhtferth's Enchiridion*, eds. Peter S. Baker and Michael Lapidge, EETS ss 15 (London: Oxford University Press, 1995).

9. Ibid., xv-xxxiv.

10. Ælfric, *Ælfric's Lives of Saints*, ed. W. W. Skeat os 76, 82, 94, 114 (London: Oxford University Press, [1881-1900] 1966), 2. 714-17 (264-65).

11. John Trevisa, *The Governance of Kings and Princes: John Trevisa's Middle English Translation of the De Regimine Principum of Aegidius Romanus*, eds. David C. Fowler, Charles F. Briggs, and Paul G. Remley (New York: Garland, 1997) II. II. XVII (242). "*And ȝif me axe how men scholde be reweled after þat age* [twenty-one, twenty-five, or twenty-seven], *for þanne þei ben icome as it were to folle perfecioun, þei scholde þanne cunne rewle himself.*" Translation: After age twenty-one, or twenty-five, or twenty-seven, men should finally—hopefully—have arrived at full

adulthood and be able to rule themselves.

12. This manuscript, Royal MS 6 E VI, is curated at the British Library. Images from the manuscript can be found at: http://www.bl.uk/catalogues/illuminatedmanuscripts/record.asp?MSID=7788&CollID=16&NStart=60506.

13. *Omne Bonum*, Royal MS 6 E VI, folio 58v. See entire page here: http://www.bl.uk/catalogues/illuminatedmanuscripts/ILLUMIN.ASP?Size=mid&IllID=41788.

14. Lucy Freeman Sandler, *Omne Bonum: A Fourteenth-Century Encyclopedia of Universal Knowledge*, 2 vols. (London: Harvey Miller Publishers, 1996), 97. There is no published transcription of the full *adolescens* entry. Those interested in medieval Latin paleography—and who wouldn't be—can see the first page here: http://www.bl.uk/catalogues/illuminatedmanuscripts/ILLUMIN.ASP?Size=mid&IllID=41788.

15. John Wilkins, *Essay Towards a Real Character and a Philosophical Language* (London: 1668).

16. The dictionaries referenced here are catalogued and digitized on the research databases Early English Books Online and Eighteenth Century Collections Online. Some of them can be freely accessed at Google books.

THE CREATORS | III

If you fancy yourself saving the world in the early twenty-first century, you might refashion yourself as a mostly-but-not-quite-fully-human human who flaunts stunningly impressive powers that are mostly-but-not-quite-fully-human standard fare. Liquifying oneself, perhaps. Or spontaneously combusting into copper-colored unicorn manes. Or obliterating a repulsive monstrosity with a casual glimpse of multi-lasered retinas. Or surviving a 48-hour middle school lock-in that features hourly dodgeball take-downs.

Vengeance is mine, saith the LORD. Avenger-ness, though, belongs to Hollywood, along with all other manner of spectacularness, so if the mostly-but-not-quite-fully-human thing isn't your cup of tea, you could instead be an extraordinary everyday adolescent female, perhaps named Katniss or Beatrice, who single-handedly manages to bring down an entire populace of nefarious adults with a single spectacular and wholly human shot / leap / berry / blow / breath / take-your-pick.

The currency of adolescent female awesomeness has recently experienced an especially strong market surge, regardless of whether that awesomeness centers around overthrowing the Capitol or overthrowing the Erudites. There's no way to know if Katniss and Beatrice will enjoy the same longstanding adoration attached to someone like Jo March or Anne Shirley. But for now, they are superstars who are hauling in superdollars for their creators and production crews.

CREATIVE REPRESENTATIONS OF *ADOLESCENTCE*

Young adult fiction, whether printed on the page or acted on the screen, is routinely and rabidly consumed by audiences of all ages. It has hit an exhilarating roller coaster stride in part because of powerful marketing machines, but also because adolescents who are bravely sticking it to the man while also navigating the journey from dependence to independence make for such fascinating, engaging, and entertaining subjects. The phenomenon is not limited to narratives, nor is it limited to our twentieth- and twenty-first-century slice of history. Long before Katniss and Beatrice—even long before Jo March and Anne Shirley—the creative output of poets and painters, storytellers and songwriters, playwrights and printers, melodramatists and musicians has featured adolescents, male and female alike.

How much those creative representations accurately reflect actual adolescent experience is quite another matter. The fact that such creative representations exist at all is what interests me here because their existence implies that society at large— not just the reclusive and intellectually minded Thinkers— has had some general ideas, theories, and opinions about *adolescentce* for a very long time.

For starters, consider the *Omne Bonum* entry for *adolescens/ adolescencia* discussed in the last chapter. In addition to the

long informational text based on the authority and wisdom
of both ancient and contemporary Thinkers, the entry also
includes a detailed historiated initial *A* into which an unnamed
artist inserted and wove his own thoughts and views of
adolescentce. You can see the illustration both here and on the
cover.

Detail of folio 58v, Royal MS 6 E VI, *Omne Bonum*. Image used by permission of the British Library, free
of copyright restrictions. Image can be found online at www.bl.uk/catalogues/illuminatedmanuscripts/
ILLUMIN.ASP?Size=mid&IllID=31840.

Take a close look. Do you see what is so obviously going on
here?

On the left side of the image an adolescent female stares into a mirror, a traditional medieval icon for both vanity and self-awareness. She hitches up her skirt, a traditional medieval (and modern) symbol of sensuality and flirtation. She is equally interested in how she looks to herself and how she looks to others, most especially That Guy.

On the right we have That Guy—a beardless adolescent male. Regardless of how tall, virile, or manly he may appear, being beardless in medieval and early modern art is a sure sign of not yet being a full adult.[1] Throughout *Omne Bonum*, illustrations of adult males including Jesus, Noah, Moses, Adam, Boaz, a judge, a lawyer, a dentist, a teacher with his pupil, a father attending his child's baptism, and a man in bed with another man's wife (entry: *adulterium*) are all bearded. They are grown. They are adults, misbehaving or otherwise. They have arrived. But not That Guy. Not our guy. Not yet.

He holds his right hand to his heart and his left on his stomach, a sure sign that he's smitten to the core; this same pose appears in the book's entry for *Cardiaco passio* or Heart Pains.[2] Most telling of all, his left hand is placed so that he can quickly unsheath his sword—and by sword I do not mean sword. Just look at the design of the pommel and the placement of the blade. I have little patience for people who see phallic symbols lurking around every corner, but this young man is obviously not headed onto the traditional battlefield.

Best of all, he is wearing medieval jeggings and TOMs. And a Katniss-like cowl.

He and she are so entirely contemporary even while they are so entirely historical. We recognize them, even if they do look a bit stiff and caricatured.

This picture, only several inches wide and high in the original, is full of interesting opinions and stereotypes.

- Adolescents are vain. It could just as easily be the male gazing into the mirror as the female. In fact it's rather a toss-up as to who wins the self-staring contest in this picture.
- Adolescents are overly concerned with fashion. The young man's tight hose and short tunic were the height of medieval hipsterhood. Mature adults often bemoaned and lampooned the adolescent and young adult males who insisted on wearing those scandalous mini-tunics. Just think of how difficult it must have been for the females to guard their eyes and hearts in the presence of such thoughtless immodesty.
- Adolescents have only one thing on their minds, namely romance that leads to sword play.

Ironically, though the written text for this entry includes many stereotypical descriptions of adolescence, the illustration does not directly represent any of them in detail. Rather, it expands and extends the representation based on the artist's own views, opinions, and experiences.

Even when considered all by itself, the *adolescens/adolescencia* entry is a stunning reality in light of today's popular narrative about adolescence and its recent construction. *Omne Bonum*—filled with practical information about religion, biology, history, animals, crops, literature, astronomy, philosophy, *and* adolescence—surely must cause us to cast a broader and more critical eye as we determine just how far back we might search for various depictions, definitions, and opinions of adolescence.

But *Omne Bonum* needn't be considered all by itself because it is only one among many historical creative representations of adolescence, just a few of which are included here.

COLORING THE "IN-BETWEEN" AGE

Almost one hundred years after *Omne Bonum*, a French translation of Bartholomaeus Anglicus' *De proprietatibus rerum* ("On the Properties of Things") was produced. The section on the seven ages of man, just like that of "adolescens/adolescencia" in *Omne Bonum*, includes a small but detailed illustration of the different ages.

Here they are: the seven ages of man (and presumably woman too).

The two little guys on the far right represent the two different stages of childhood, up to age seven and up to age fourteen. The youngest plays with a toy while the next oldest carries a schoolbook. Their faces admittedly do not look very childlike, but art back then was more symbolic than realistic. Their relative sizes indicates their age and their various levels of social importance.[3]

The four guys on the left represent the different stages of full adulthood. Notice their modest maxi-dress-like tunics. Though not apparent in this black and white rendering, the landscape behind the two oldest is brown, withered, and lifeless (while the landscape on the right is vibrant and green). The juices of youth have begun to dry up, not just in the men but also in the earth.

Now look at the guy in the middle, striking a pose and copping an attitude of what—aloofness? disdain? superiority? machismo?—that masks what—insecurity? angst? confusion? pride? That Guy is our beloved adolescent. He is wearing green, the color of youth. He is physically well-endowed, indicating his sexual maturity; but he is beardless, indicating his lack of full adulthood. He is taller than the children, but not yet as tall as the adults, indicating both his relative age and social status. He

Detail of folio 139v, Royal MS 15 E II, *De Proprietatibus Rerum* in French (*Livre des proprietez des Choses*). Image used by permission of the British Library, free of copyright restrictions. Image can be found online at www.bl.uk/catalogues/illuminatedmanuscripts/ILLUMIN.ASP?Size=mid&IllID=29422.

looks down on the kiddos and away from the adults, indicating his attitude toward both. He belongs to neither group fully. He exists in his own in-between space.

And in case you missed it, he is wearing an extremely short tunic that leaves nothing to the imagination and carrying an oversized sword, though like That Other Guy in *Omne Bonum* he is neither armed nor dressed for an actual battle.

Best of all, he is wearing medieval leggings and TOMs. Instead of a Katniss-cowl, he wears what looks like the top of a bamboo rice steamer on his head, trendsetter that he is.

Aside from these and other artist renderings of specific age groups within a larger life cycle, adolescents were rarely featured front and center in paintings or illustrations. In fact, they were marginalized, literally—shoved to the outer edges of many manuscripts and books—where they are most often shown with peers, doing all kinds of typically adolescent things: flirting, goofing off, fighting, shopping, preening, being disruptive, and engaging in such things as "breaking wind" (as the more genteel folk preferred to call it) and drinking games.[4]

The visual representations of adolescence are striking and colorful, and I encourage you to look them up online and see them in their full glory. But so are the written descriptions and depictions.[5] Chaucer loved to write about adolescents and young adults and has been called the author of youth[6] and the "disciple and poet" of Venus.[7] You may remember that Venus is the planet believed to influence and control adolescents and young adults. In his *Canterbury Tales* alone, adolescents and young adults fill the pages: Arcita, Palamon, and Emelye form a convoluted love triangle in the Knight's Tale; Perkyn of the Cook's Tale, an apprentice who has almost finished his contract, has a hipster hairstyle, loves to party on the weekends, and leans toward riotous and girl-chasing behavior, much to has master's dismay; Nicholas, Alison, Absolon, John, Aleyne, May, and Damien (from the Miller's, Reeve's, and Merchant's Tales) are stereotypically sex-crazed, vain, and disdainful of adults; and the "rioutous youths" of the Pardoner's Tale are just that—singing, dancing, gambling, drinking, irresponsible, lazy, vain, lust-filled, good-for-nothing not-yet-full-adults. Besides the characters themselves, Chaucer describes paintings of adolescents that adorn Venus' temple, a space that figures largely in the Knight's Tale. The images feature: disrupted sleep, deep sighs, tears and lamenting; burning strokes of the desires that define this age; pleasure, hopes, desire, and foolhardiness; beauty, youth, baudery, charms, flattery, busyness, and jealousy; parties, music, singing, and dancing; lust and wild behavior; and all the other things that go along with adolescent passion and love.[8] Indeed.

Shakespeare, too, wrote about adolescents—Romeo and Juliet come to mind, angst-ridden teen crushes who act without thinking while still technically living under the control of their elders. And in *Much Ado About Nothing*, there is Beatrice's comment: "He that hath a beard is more than a youth, and he that hath no beard is less than a man."[9]

ODES TO *ADOLESCENTCE*: FURTHER CREATIVE DEPICTIONS

Popular poets and songwriters loved adolescent characters— including students, apprentices, and fair maidens who were sometimes superlatively virtuous and other times despicably debauched. They starred in many of the cheap and popular broadsheet ballads of the fifteenth and sixteenth centuries[10] that told of young love, unrequited love, disobedient teenagers, rebellious students, angst-ridden maidens, moody striplings, and lots of unplanned out-of-wedlock pregnancies.

One of these ballads, about an adolescent apprentice named George Barnwell, proved so popular that it was refashioned into a story, a novelette, and a stage play. The earliest ballad version was titled "An Excellent Ballad of George Barnwell, an Apprentice in the City of London, Who Was Undone by a Strumpet, Who Caused Him Thrice to Rob His Master, and to Murder His Uncle in Ludlow."[11] Written for "all youths of fair England," it was a two-page condensed tale of young George being seduced by an older woman—much like Joseph and Potiphar, though George lacked Joseph's self-control. The longer story version, *The 'Prentice's Tragedy: or, The History of George Barnwell Being a Fair Warning to Young Men to Avoid the Company of Lewd Women* is full of riotous living, ruffians, and inexperienced youth.[12] The preface to the stage adaptation says it is a moral tale intended to warn and shame thoughtless youth from destructive bad behavior. In this version, George's age is given: He is eighteen and hasn't yet thought of marriage because of his "youth and circumstances."[13] Yet another narrative version, *Youth's Warning Piece: The Tragical History of George Barnwell* describes George as a "giddy inexperienced youth" with "frail resolve" who requires the oversight of an adult in order to toe the line.[14]

George Barnwell (among many other literary, dramatic, and musical characters throughout the centuries) represents all stereotyped teens who fall into trouble because they lack life experience, self-control, and common sense—and because they refuse to listen to the adults in their lives. Whether George Barnwell is real or not isn't the issue. The fact that George Barnwell exists even just as a creative representation says something about the history of adolescence—namely that adults have had views, opinions, and ideas about it for a very long time.

Almost a hundred years before George Barnwell became the

face of easily-seduced adolescence, four other characters, also apprentices, were the face of heroic and courageous youth, a sort of prequel to the *Divergent* and *Hunger Games* dynasties. *The Foure Prentises of London*[15] was dedicated to "the honest and *hie*-spirited Prentises, the Readers." Seeing as apprentices at this time in history were generally between the ages of sixteen and young-twenties,[16] this could reasonably be categorized as late-Renaissance young adult dramatic fiction. In the play, four adolescent brothers—Godfrey, Guy, Charles, and Eustace, from oldest to youngest—have been apprenticed out to various tradesmen based on their individual personalities and abilities: mercer, goldsmith, haberdasher, and grocer (respectively). We are often told that before the nineteenth century, youth as a rule followed in their parents' footsteps. But in both literature and life, there are many examples of just the opposite. Many adolescents had an array of choices and options regarding apprenticeships. Some of those options were more expensive and carried more status, a sort of Ivy League apprenticeship track. Others were less expensive and closer to home, so were more realistic options for families with limited funds and fewer connections.

In the opening lines of the play, the youngest son Eustace complains to his father that his master monitors his free time too closely, doesn't let him spend enough time with his friends, and doesn't let him enjoy the weekend the way he would like, namely by "strik[ing] a footeballe in the streete," going to a wrestling contest, or just hanging out doing nothing. These are the things that Eustace—apprentice for just two years, so very likely between fourteen and eighteen years old—wants and expects to do, but he is pushed too hard (in his opinion) to learn and perform. His master is always on his case, calling his name every chance he gets, and not allowing him even "one howre for sport." All four apprentices long for a life of adventure, free from the drudgery of learning, menial-task jobs, and adult supervision. In true Hollywood fashion, that is exactly what they find, and in the end they prove that if an adolescent or young adult can simply shake off the oppressive shackles of adult-controlled adolescent life, they can remake themselves as heroes in a star-studded fashion. Along the way, they rescue, save, and defend all kinds of folk and make a memorable name for themselves.

If George Barnwell was the quintessential irresponsible and sex-crazed youth, the four apprentices-turned-superheroes were the quintessential idealized saintly youths. As often happens even still today, most adolescent characters several centuries ago were either unrealistically idealized or stereotypically demonized.

While George Barnwell was ripping up England (both old and New, for there is ample evidence of the play being performed in Boston), a far less dramatic view of adolescence appeared in a New Haven, Connecticut, publication. *A Survey of Man from the Cradle to the Grave: A Poem* rolled off the presses in 1760.[17] The Youth, introduced after the child and then the boy, may sound familiar. He desperately wants a girl, so badly that he is "disconsolate and sick." He truly believes that a girlfriend "will complete his bliss," only to find that when things fall apart, he is left "aghast, deceived, perhaps undone." Fortunately, the next girlfriend is better than the first, a lass who "surpasses all the shining stars." He's whipped. He drowns in youthful lust. He has found true love at last. The poet concludes this section with: "Thus passes Youth, 'till Manhood takes its place."

Manhood is described as a time of business, job, and wider society. The next logical step is marriage. He finally understands what real love and genuine relationship is, as opposed to the foolish lust and passions of youth. He eventually becomes a parent. His children grow into adolescence, a "gaudy stripling" and a "mincing dame" who waver about life, wait idly for their future destiny to announce itself, have high opinions of themselves, assume they are more rational than anyone else, and want to make their own decisions. The poet's assessment of the son? "Poor beardless boy!" His friends laugh at his jokes and tell him he's awesome while he acts like he owns the world. Meanwhile the daughter is caught up in her outer appearance. Both parents worry and struggle through anxious days and restless nights while the kids are out late. They lie awake in bed, fretting, fuming, unable to sleep, consumed with worry. All they want is for their children to finally grow up, settle down, create adult lives, marry, and start families of their own. Thus were parents of adolescents described in the 1700s.

A similar description of adolescence can be found two hundred years earlier in *Mundus et Infans* (The World and the Child), a morality play of the early sixteenth century.[18] The main character progresses through all the different stages of life and gets a new name at each stage of the journey. He is called *Infans* up to age seven, then *Wanton* up to age fourteen. Wanton plays with a spinning top; hits his friends on the head with a stick; scratches, bites, kicks, and mocks his siblings; pouts if his parents threaten punishment; calls his mother names; lies; dances, skips, whistles, and plays cherry pit; steals fruit from neighbors' gardens while walking to school; and other boyish things.

At age fourteen, Wanton—sort of like Abram, Jacob, Simon, and Saul before him (but really not like that at all)—gets a new name that perfectly describes his new identity. He is now known as Love, Lust, and Liking—soon shortened to just Lust and Liking, which probably says a lot about how the author viewed adolescence. The new name is given, we are told, because of that age's natural tendencies towards lewdness. Lust and Liking dives into his new identity with full confidence, knowing he is fresh as May flowers, good-looking, well-dressed, appealing to the ladies, and ready for a life of pleasure-seeking and rioting.

When he turns twenty-one, Lust and Liking gets yet another new name: Manhood. But things don't go as planned. For a number of years, he refuses to grow up, settle down, and give up the trappings of adolescence. He delays adult responsibility, makes poor decisions, and remains focused on only himself. He emerges into adulthood ever so slowly, and not completely even then because being named Manhood is not necessarily the same thing as actually being a man.

Interestingly, the title page of the 1522 edition of *The World and the Child* indicates that the play intends to show the nature of childhood and manhood.[19] Some might argue that the subtitle is proof that way back then, people were considered either a child or an adult. If so, then adolescence—or Lust and Liking as the playwright would have it—is part of childhood along with Infans and Wanton since the name Manhood is not bestowed until age twenty-one, *after* adolescence. Or maybe the subtitle, like many other things in life, assumes that readers understand the phrase childhood-and-manhood as referring to the total arc of life and not to a simple binary view of the human journey.

INCLINED TO FOLLY AND FRIVOLITY

Adolescents weren't just created characters; they were also Creators themselves. The most striking example of this goes way back to the early Middle Ages when a group of young university students churned out songs that would make Becky blush. (If you don't know her, "Becky" is the target audience of Christian radio, a socially constructed persona; she is between thirty and forty, probably married with kids; she enjoys listening to male singers croon about Jesus.)[20]

These young men, many of whom were second or third sons in a world that favored first sons, bounced from school to school in pursuit of whatever knowledge could be gained at each particular institution.[21] Perhaps they enjoyed the thrill of learning. Perhaps they enjoyed the sense of adventure. Perhaps they couldn't settle on a single major. Perhaps they enjoyed the unencumbered freedom. Perhaps they had nothing better to do than fritter away their time.

In today's Western culture, these young men would have been high school and college aged—adolescents, young adults, or emerging adults in our lexicon. They were sometimes far from home, not yet settled down and not yet engaged in a single stable career. Contemporaries most often described them as lighthearted, careless, pleasure-seeking, and disreputable. They were their own demographic. They had equal disdain for both crude commoners and stuffy sell-outs, viewing themselves as more intellectual than the former and more clever than the latter.

Primarily, they drank a lot. Thus is their musical corpus most often referred to as simply Drinking Songs. The most popular topics are (no surprise) drinking, women, rebellion, and sticking it to the man. As you can imagine, the songs much like the students were viewed with either deep disdain or wild applause.

Isn't that always how it is? At least to some degree? There are those who adore adolescence—its vigor, adventure, passion, energy, enthusiasm, zest, and wit. And there are those who abhor adolescence—its attitude, instability, rage, lust, skepticism, defiance, moodiness, rebellion, sarcasm.

They are great. They are awful. They are wondrous. They are trouble. Back and forth we go, swinging the pendulum from one extreme to the other, relegating adolescents to the far extremes—where only a very few people exist—rather than to the larger and more expansive center, where most of humanity finds itself.

Even in a popular fourteenth-century religious poem, *A Stanzaic Life of Christ*, adolescence makes an appearance.[22] It is described as the age from fourteen to twenty-eight. It is inclined to folly and frivolity, the age most likely to make bad choices and do bad things. And none of this, says the poet, should be a surprise to anyone. Just look around. It's obvious to anyone who has ever known an adolescent.

Such views of adolescence are not new, which is not to say they are accurate. Rather, it is to say that there is a longstanding and recurring reality of how adults view *adolescentce* and how those views might pass from one generation to the next. One brief example will make the point.

"The Zodiac of Life," a sixteenth-century English translation of a contemporary Latin poem, was commonly used in the grammar school education of English students, one of whom was quite probably William Shakespeare. The poem described the various ages of man, including this about adolescence:

> Then lusty youth approaching comes,
>   and strength increases fair.
> Now from his mouth he shakes the bit,
>   now counsel none he hears,
> He rages now with furious mode,
>   and burns in youthful years,
> With rage and riot runs he mad,
>   and rash without advice,
> No counsel will he take therein,
>   but witty words despise.

No dangers does he now esteem
    so he the thing obtain,
Whereto lascivious lust him moves
    and force of willful brain.
Neglecting laws he brawls and fights
    and brainsick runs astray,
The greatest part of youth are now
    with passions led away.
A few whom fear or shamefastness
    or wisdom does restrain,
Their youthful days uprightly lead
    and void of vicious stain.[23]

Modern translation of the Middle English translation of the
Old French original: most adolescents are bad. Very bad. A few
are good. Very good. The very bad sound entirely dreary and
debauched, which was exactly the point per the book's subtitle:

> *Wherein are contained twelve books disclosing the
> heinous crimes [and] wicked vices of our corrupt nature:
> and plainly declaring the pleasant and perfect pathway
> unto eternal life, besides a number of digressions both
> pleasant [and] profitable.*

There's nothing quite like an old subtitle to give away the true
tone and intent of a book.

Shakespeare scholars agree that he was familiar with *Zodiac's*
content. Writing forty or so years after it was first published,
Shakespeare himself pontificated on the seven ages of man in
As You Like It, showing briefly how the baton of adolescent
representation was sometimes passed:

> All the world's a stage,
> And all the men and women merely players.

They have their exits and their entrances,
And one man in his time plays many parts,
His acts being seven ages. At first the infant,
Mewling and puking in the nurse's arms.
Then, the whining school-boy with his satchel
And shining morning face, creeping like snail
Unwillingly to school. And then the lover,
Sighing like furnace, with a woeful ballad
Made to his mistress' eyebrow. Then, a soldier,
Full of strange oaths, and bearded like the pard,
Jealous in honour, sudden, and quick in quarrel,
Seeking the bubble reputation
Even in the cannon's mouth. And then, the justice,
In fair round belly, with a good capon lined,
With eyes severe, and beard of formal cut,
Full of wise saws, and modern instances,
And so he plays his part. The sixth age shifts
Into the lean and slippered pantaloon,
With spectacles on nose and pouch on side,
His youthful hose, well saved, a world too wide
For his shrunk shank, and his big manly voice,
Turning again toward childish treble, pipes
And whistles in his sound. Last scene of all,
That ends this strange eventful history,
Is second childishness and mere oblivion,
Sans teeth, sans eyes, sans taste, sans everything
— Act II, Scene VII

Here adolescence is reduced to the angst of romantic relationships—which sounds so very Shakespearian—and so for at least another generation, the stereotyped descriptions were renewed and replenished.

These examples of how Creators envisioned and then represented adolescence over the past several centuries are just a sliver of the historical record. Once the novel comes into full swing in the late eighteenth century (give or take a few decades, depending on who you ask), adolescence is represented on an even larger scale by many authors, which then leads into the *Bildungsroman* (the standard coming-of-age narrative) that has come to define the genre for many readers. It is arguably the most common and beloved reading fare, the quintessential storyline that speaks to the soul of almost every reader who watches the protagonist grow socially, psychologically, emotionally, and spiritually from adolescence into adulthood.

Ironically, the novel is also one of the art forms most heartily denounced by the Preachers who feared the negative effects that such creative output would have on the still developing souls and identities of adolescents.

And so to the Preachers we go.

ENDNOTES

1. See Robert Bartlett, "Symbolic Meanings of Hair in the Middle Ages," *Transactions of the Royal Historical Society* 4 (1994), 43-60 at 43-44; Will Fisher, "The Renaissance Beard: Masculinity in Early Modern England," *Renaissance Quarterly* 54 (2001), 155-187.
2. Folio 239 of *Omne Bonum*. The young male in that illustration is beardless, wears a short tunic and tight leggings, and holds his hands just as That Guy does. The only difference is that he is alone, *sans* young maiden, and is sitting down, "unarmed" so to speak.
3. Michel Pastoureau, "Emblems of Youth: Young People in Medieval Imagery," in *A History of Young People in the West: Ancient and Medieval Rites of Passage*, eds. Giovanni Levi and Jean-Claude Schmitt, trans. Camille Naish (Cambridge, MA: Belknap Press of Harvard University Press, 1997), 222-39 at 229-230. "To depict old men as very large and young men as very small—when in reality men and women of eighteen to twenty are often larger than those of sixty or eighty—amounts to using imagery to proclaim a clear difference in status, be it social, theological, political, juridical, economic, or symbolic. A young man occupies a small place in an image because he occupied a small place in society."
4. Pastoureau, 231-233. For some colorful and vivid examples of marginal illustrations, many featuring children and adolescents, check out the *Roman d'Alexandre*, curated at the Bodleian Library, with free online access. The whole manuscript is available here: http://image.ox.ac.uk/show-all-openings?collection=bodleian&manuscript=msbodl264.
5. For a survey of additional authors than those mentioned here, see Claudio Violato and Arthur J. Wiley, "Images of Adolescence in English Literature: The Middle Ages to the Modern Period," *Adolescence* XXV (Summer 1990), 253-264.
6. Howard Rollin Patch, "Chaucer and Youth," *College English* 1 (1949), 14-22 at 15.
7. John Gower, *Confessio Amantis*, ed. Russell A. Peck (Toronto: University of Toronto Press, [1966] 1980), 522.
8. Chaucer, *Riverside Chaucer*, I. A. 1920-28, 1931-33.
9. William Shakespeare, *Much Ado About Nothing*, Act II, Scene 1, lines 36-37.
10. See Tessa Watt, *Cheap Print and Popular Piety, 1550-1640* (Cambridge, Cambridge University Press, 1991); *A Collection of Black-Letter Ballads and Broadsides, Printed in the Reign of Queen Elizabeth, Between the Years 1559 and 1597* (London: Joseph Lilly, 1867).

11. London, 1705.
12. London: printed by W. O. No date.
13. George Lillo, *The London Merchant: or The History of George Barnwell.* Second edition. (London: J. Gray, 1731). There are also late 1700s playbills for Boston productions of the play.
14. London: Printed and Sold in Aldermary Church Yard. No date.
15. Thomas Heywood. Printed at London for I. W., 1615. The play had first been acted some sixteen years earlier, when Heywood was likely in his early to mid-twenties.
16. The age and duration of apprenticeships shifted throughout history, both in Europe and America, in response to market demands, population changes, and locale. What didn't shift was the power of adults to keep adolescents out of the workforce. For a more complete treatment of apprenticeships see the Barbara Hanawalt sources used throughout the book as well as the Steven Smith titles included in the Additional Sources on page 137.
17. *A Survey of Man from the Cradle to the Grave: A Poem.* (New Haven, CT, 1760).
18. *The Worlde and the Chylde*, eds. Clifford Davidson and Peter Happé (Kalamazoo, MI: Medieval Institute Publications, 1999).
19. "Here begynneth a propre newe interlude of the worlde and the chylde, otherwyse called Mundus a[nd] infans a[nd] it sheweth of the estate of chyldehodde and manhode." Wynken de Worde, 1522.
20. "Becky" has become rather famous lately. You can read an early introduction to her here: http://www.christianitytoday.com/ct/2007/januaryweb-only/whatsupwithradio2.html.
21. See John Addington Symonds, *Wine, Women and Song: Students' Songs of the Middle Ages* (Dover Publications, 2002).
22. Frances Allen Foster, ed. *A Stanzaic Life of Christ.* EETS os 166, 1926 (Reprint, New York: Kraus, 1971).
23. Marcellus Pallingenius Stellatus, *The Zodiac of Life*, trans. Barnabe Googe. Imprinted at London by Henry Denham, for Rafe Newberye dwelling in Fleete Streate, 1565. Spelling updated and normalized.

THE PREACHERS | IV

If the Thinkers of the past *defined* and *described* adolescence
and the Creators *depicted* adolescents, it would be fair to
say that the Preachers took it one step further by *defining,
describing, depicting,* and then also *denouncing*—sometimes
even *damning*—adolescence for being an inherently wicked
and dangerous age, and adolescents themselves for being an
inherently debauched and disobedient demographic (which
wasn't a word until 1867 but was certainly a thing long before
that). Preachers viewed lust, rebellion, skepticism, faithlessness,
narcissism, pleasure-seeking, idleness, and vanity as the natural
and expected behaviors of those who had finally passed out of
childhood but hadn't yet fully crossed into adulthood.

Using twenty-first-century eyes to read sermons-of-old can
be challenging. Those that were for or about *adolescentce* can
sound gallingly harsh to modern ears, composed of what seems
superlatively narrow-minded, judgmental, vitriolic, loveless,
and patronizing rhetoric, topped with a generous dose of
grown-up *nyah-nyah-nyah*-ness. At least that's what the juiciest

bits sound like.

From *An Exhortation to Youth to Prepare for Judgment. A Sermon Occasion'd by the Late Repentance and Funeral of a Young Man*
Of all others, young persons are most apt to neglect the fear of God and be unmindful of the Maker through the temptation of sensual pleasures and youthful lusts ... their age is most inviting to the Devil to bend his chiefest forces against them, rather than against children, or aged persons, the former not being capable of making a choice, and the latter being fix'd and resolv'd in their way; his principal endeavors therefore are levell'd against youth, to draw off their hearts from God and holy things, and to divert their thoughts from the consideration of death and judgment, which would otherwise restrain and check them in pursuit of their lusts.

~ Unknown (1681, p. 12-14)

But as with all things, context is key.[1] Social, political, and cultural events surely had an impact on what Preachers said about *adolescentce*, and there is no way to ever fully know all the contextual details of a specific sermon. Even without knowing all of those details though, the galling harshness is greatly softened just by reading the sermons in their entirety, because even the most damnably vitriolic statements about *adolescentce* are embedded in sermons that were not ultimately vitriolic deep down at their cores. It was not all doom and gloom for the Preachers, nor was it all judgment and condemnation. In fact, there was and is an incredible amount of promise and hope in the words of Preachers-of-old.

The Thinkers' and Creators' words and images in the previous chapters help fill out the historical narrative in part because of how they intersect with literature, culture, scientific advancements, social theories, and other details of the day. The Preachers' words and ideas touch on those things too, but only insofar as they affect and influence the spiritual formation of youth in general and youth in their particular congregations. Preachers were deeply concerned that their adolescent congregants were engaging in lascivious dancing, *et al.*, on a regular basis; but they were infinitely more concerned about the state of their souls. In other words, bad behavior was a rhetorical target, but converted hearts were the spiritual goal.

Fair warning: This chapter makes some broad and generalized statements regarding what Preachers believed and said about youth (see the first paragraph of this chapter, for example). Obviously there are always exceptions to broad and generalized statements. So in what follows, "Preachers said" and "Preachers believed" and "Preachers thought" should all be translated as "many Preachers said" and "lots of Preachers believed" and "a number of Preachers thought." The broad and generalized statements are not disingenuously hyperbolic simply to make a point. Nor are they pulled out of thin air. They are based on real words of real preachers in real sermons delivered to real congregations and read by real people. That's a whole lot of real. We would do well to pay attention.

From *A New-Years Gift for Youth. Being the Substance of a Sermon, Preached at the Funeral of M. Elizabeth Bell, Aged Sixteen Years, Odd Months*

Look abroad into the world: consider the generality of our youth in this age, what they are, what manner of lives they lead, how vain, lewd, and debauched the most are in their conversation; how rare it is to find one amongst many that is solid, sober, and religious, that makes real conscience of avoiding all known sin, and of performing holy duties, or of exercising himself to godliness, as becomes his Christian profession. Nay, do not many of them walk, and act, and talk more like atheists, or infidels, than Christians ...

~ Samuel Peck (1686, p. 3-4)

During the past decade of searching for adolescence, I have uncovered nearly 5000 distinct pre-nineteenth-century documents that have the word *sermon* in the title and the word *youth* in the main text.[2] Even after eliminating those sermons where *youth* is used in general rather than specific terms,[3] and even after allowing for a certain percentage of database overlap, reprintings, and updated editions, there are still many, many hundreds of pre-nineteenth-century sermons that deal with adolescence specifically and several thousand that mention or refer to it. Preachers also published essays, lessons, letters, manuals, and other documents that do not use *sermon* in the title, so the total number of Preacher-generated documents is in fact even higher.

True confession: I have not read all of the sermons I have cataloged. Yet. It takes a while to read 500 years' worth of documents. But I have read more than enough to confidently make at least two assertions.

ASSERTION 1: Preachers-of-Old were well aware of adolescence as a distinct life stage.

I assume they were also well aware of particular adolescents in their communities and congregations, else they would have had little to say on the subject and no one to say it to.

Youth was the Preachers' word of choice when referring to adolescents, much like today. We have Youth Groups, not Adolescent Associations. We hire Youth Pastors, not Adolescent

Advisors. We go to Youth Camps, not Adolescent Adventures. We call our larger demographic Youth Workers, not Adolescent Coaches.

From *The Vanity of Childhood and Youth, Wherein the Depraved Nature of Young People Is Represented and Means for Their Reformation Proposed. Being Some Sermons Preached in Hand-Alley, at the Request of Several Young Men.* Young people are subject to fleshly lusts, especially uncleanness. This concerns persons past childhood, and therefore I direct it to young men. You are not ignorant that your appetites are unruly, and your inclinations too lascivious. In eating, you are prone to gluttony: excessive drinking is too common a fault; there be many drunkards short of twenty years old; and voluptuousness seems the idol whom our striplings worship above the living God. Uncleanness is the raging disease: What immodest dalliance, what flighty thoughts, what obscene speeches, what wanton looks, self-pollution; yea, actual fornication, doth conscience charge some of you with! How few possess their vessels in honour, or arrive at Manhood without a forfeiture of chastity!

~ Daniel Williams (1691, p. 55)

Though the Preachers did not use the English terms *adolescence* or *adolescency* with great frequency, they did often use the Latin term to pound home a point, Latin being the language of authority and therefore useful for pounding. In a 1615 sermon describing Satan's best strategies for bringing down humanity, listeners were told that Satan grudgingly allows adults to follow their religious inclinations but he claims youth for his own:

This is the Devil's dispensation, *Youth must be born with,* to dance, to dice, to drink, to ruffle, scuffle, wear fleeces of vanity on their heads, and to leave no place without some vicious testimony of their presence, *non est vitium adolescenti,* is no fault in a man.[4] (original italics)

There you have it. Dancing, gambling, drinking, rioting, and vain pride combine to be an adolescent's birthright, compliments of the Devil. It is inevitable. It cannot be helped. It is a phase of life. It will pass (if all goes as it should) when someone finally crosses the threshold of adulthood. Therefore *non est vitium adolescenti* (there is no fault for a young person), though certainly the offenses are very real.

At least that's how the soundbite reads. But the larger context reveals something else entirely, namely that these natural tendencies towards vice, though very real, are not inevitable. Instead, "it is good to begin at the gates of our life to serve God." Otherwise "the frame of our lives be built on a lascivious and riotous foundation of long-practiced lasciviousness, our bones be full of the sin of our youth." Sorry, Satan: "All the degrees of our life shall be devoted to the service of God."[5]

From *A Sure Guide to Hell—By Beelzebub*
We may now suppose thee arrived at the age of fifteen or sixteen—many are the youths who have gone [to the university] with good purposes of improving themselves in useful knowledge and establishing themselves in virtuous habits; but so far have they been from effecting the design that I have, by the many agents who do my business there, seduced them to the practice of almost every vice; such as drunkenness, whoredom, profaneness, swearing, [etc.] ...

~ Benjamin Bourne writing as Belial (1775, p. 17)

The hopeful light at the end of the tunnel—even in the midst of the tunnel—was very real to the Preachers. But so was the dark tunnel to which adolescents were drawn, or from which they descended—depending on one's view. They had a "combustible nature and constitution" so naturally the devil "night and day is watching to set fire to [their] lusts."[6] This type of description is quite common in sermons-of-old.

Not only did Preachers have an awareness of adolescence as a stage of life, but their assumptions, ideas, and fears about adolescents remained fairly consistent over the centuries. For starters, sermons to and about *adolescentce* almost always presumed that the present era was more dangerous and wicked than the previous one and that the increased danger and wickedness impacted adolescents more than anyone else. "Times are terrible—more terrible than the terrible of our ancestors" was the repeated mantra. Preachers (and perhaps parents, teachers, and other authority figures) were sure that however much the youth may have been dancing, dicing, drinking, and rioting in the previous generation, the youths of the current generation were doing all those things in greater measure. And why wouldn't they? Culture was a mess. The songs were dirtier, the plays were bawdier, the novels were lustier, and the local merchants were intent on sucking the pockets of adolescents dry. That's right: adolescents shopped, long before malls and second-day delivery.

In the fifteenth century, people may not have talked about a market-driven economy, but they sure did talk about the market. One Preacher specifically noted that fourteen- to eighteen-year-olds loved to hang out at the markets and fairs, perusing the "merchandise of the devil." They, more than any other age group, were especially prone to blow their cash on hipster designer apparel—short collars from Germany; "evil-fashioned" garments and "devilish" shoes and slippers from France; bags and pouches from Spain; and stylish hats from Italy.[7] That might have been because those same fourteen- to eighteen-year-olds were "full of undevotion," often forgetting to worship God (and the saints), and even "if he do it with his mouth, his heart is full far from God about worldly vanities."[8]

Translation: Their faith—assuming they had any—tended towards shallow rather than deep, often extending no further than their words.

From *Two Discourses Addressed to Young Persons: To which is added, A Sermon Occasioned by the Earthquake, which was October 29, 1727*
Young persons have their hearts so much set upon their pleasures …They are ready to think that this and the other carnal joy and sensual pleasure must be gratified: and they are prone vainly to imaging that if they should become sober and virtuous, they should be tied up to such straight rules as never more to know what pleasure means …

~ John Barnard (1727, p. 14)

The reasoning was a bit chicken-and-eggish. Shallow faith perhaps caused a desire to continually acquire newer and better things. At the same time, it resulted in part from the lure of worldly entertainments, which Preachers worried were a bigger draw for adolescents than the Church. "A merry tale will more affect them, romances, plays and comedies, such bubbles, and empty vanity are much more pleasing, than the most powerful heavenly sermon."[9] Historical Preachers may not have made the strategic move to emulate worldly entertainments by giving them a Jesus-spin, but they certainly were aware of the crosshairs in which their youth found themselves.

Entertainment was only part of the problem. Another major lure away from faithful church attendance, and by extension a deep and abiding faith, was sports, which included all kinds of games and activities, including football. Not the American

version. The original version. You know: s-o-c-c-e-r.
If the Preachers spoke truth, adolescent males were forever
despoiling the Sabbath day by skipping church and heading out
to the athletic field. In 1636, a preacher claimed that youth were
skipping church so much that it "increased and surpassed our
fathers' sins."[10] (Translation: Times are terrible-times-ten.)

Preacher's blamed the trouble in part on a 1618 king's
declaration about sports that could lawfully be played on
Sunday, after church. It seems that the "after church" part
eventually got lost in the ruckus, and though the original
declaration hadn't been just for youth, it was youth who took
the encouragement and ran with it and youth who bore the
brunt of the Preachers' scoldings. They skipped church to swim
on Sunday, to play football on Sunday, to enjoy May-games on
Sunday. "So manifold mischiefs have attended and followed,
as never any age since Christ, much less such a Christian state
as we profess to be, hath seen, or ever heard the like ... [the
book] inhibits Magistrates and superiors, to restrain or punish
youth for taking such liberty on the Lord's day, as the book
alloweth, and which *all other* books, writing, monuments of
fathers, councils, kings, emperors, divines ancient and modern,
protestants and papists, have universally with one vote and
voice cried down, til now but yesterday a new generation of
maleferiati hath risen up, out-daring and defying the whole
world and God himself."[11] (Translation: Times are terrible-
times-a-thousand.)

God does not entertain *maleferiati*, and so in his eminent
wisdom and justice, those adolescents who chose to skip church
to play football did so at their own peril as evidenced by the fact
that on at least one occasion, such *maleferiati* fell through the
ice to their deaths. God loved youth but had little patience with
those who mocked his holy day.

Severall young men playing at foote-ball
on the Ice upon the Lords-day are all Drownd

© The British Library Board. General Reference Collection 816.m.22.(50)

Detail from *Divine Examples of God's Severe Judgments upon Sabbath-Breakers, in Their Unlawful Sports, Collected out of Several Divine Subjects*. London: Printed for T. C. and sold by William Miller, at the Sign of the Gilded Acorn in St. Paul's Church-Yard, near the Little North Door, 1671. Image published with permission of ProQuest. Further reproduction is prohibited without permission. Image produced by ProQuest as part of *Early English Books Online*. www.proquest.com

Even up to 1810, slightly beyond the date of most sermons considered here, sports were a serious problem. "Sports of the field constitute the last source of youthful enjoyments which will be noticed. By these I mean chiefly the sports of the turf, as they are called, which collect a host of idlers and gamblers; cherish habits of dissipation and extravagance; waste precious time, for which an account must be rendered to God; and enfeeble the restraints of morality and religion."[12]

From *A Directory for Youth*
Youth is prone to Sabbath breaking; a day which usually young people meet together upon, to walk abroad in the fields, and take their pleasure, and run into all excess of riot, chambering, acting their filthy lusts, drinking healths, playing at cards, dancing, swearing, and sometimes quarrelling, fighting, thieving, robbing of orchards and gardens, and thus inverting the day which God hath sanctified, and appropriated to his own honour and service, and the saving of souls, to the service of the Devil, and damning their own souls.

~ Samuel Pomfret (1693, p. 23-24)

Skipping church to hang out with friends was just one of many concerns Preachers had about adolescents. Many sermons included full lists of adolescent ills. For example:

1. "Some are disorderly in the night time. Parents make them work diligently in the daytime; but in the evening they gather together in companies, and spend their time in unprofitable talk ... Is this for the praise of the name of God, that when the family go to bed, the young man is running about the town?"
2. Some of them hang out at the bars, "swaggering and vaporing," wasting what little money they've earned, instead of staying at home where they belong and will be safe.
3. Some are given to wanton dalliances—"Men and maids will be in company together, toying and dallying; they are stirring up corruption in one another ... They go to meeting on the Sabbath day and at night they are sporting with one another."[13]

Here is another longer list of "sins that hang about, that haunt, and dog that season of life":

1. Airiness of spirit, levity of mind, vanity of thoughts.
2. Blind boldness in adventuring on desperately, in dangerous ways.
3. Careless incogitancy and inconsiderateness about the most awful important matters of their souls.
4. Delaying repentance and turning to God, foolishly thinking it's time enough, they are yet young.
5. Eager pursuits after sensual pleasures, games, etc. Loving these more than God.
6. Flexibility to temptations, as dry tinder to receive the least spark, easily enticed.
7. Going down the stream and doing as a multitude of other young people do.
8. Hating instructions, admonition, and reproof.
9. Intemperance in meats and drinks.
10. Keeping of ill company, that soul-ruining snare of hell.
11. Lying and inventing excuses.
12. Making little or no conscience of relative duties.
13. Nourishing vain hopes, and flattering themselves with the thoughts of long life, and putting far away the evil day.
14. Omitting the holy observation of the Sabbath.
15. Pride of their parts, beauty, strength.
16. Quenching the motions of the Holy Spirit
17. Ridiculing serious religion as too strict and more than needs.
18. Time-wasting.
19. Uncleanness. (Code for: sex.)
20. Woeful giddiness of spirit, ready to imbibe any kind of error.[14]

That pretty much covers it, except to add that as a rule, youth are (in this particular Preacher's humble opinion) "light spirited and frothy." Like a refreshing summer drink.

ASSERTION 2: Preachers recognized the role of the Church—both actual (for good or ill) and ideal—in the lives of adolescents.

In terms of youth becoming disinterested in religion or leaving the Church, culture has always been and continues to be an easy target. Preachers-of-old knew culture wasn't the sole culprit, however. At least some of them believed the Church itself—or at least youth's perception of the Church—bore part of the blame. Adolescents (said the Preachers)—with their "affected boldness and courage"—were neither impressed nor drawn to religion that was expressed as timidity or shyness, which apparently it often was. Consequently, rather than defending the faith against sin and ridicule, adolescents did just the opposite: "Instead of being ashamed of *folly* and *vice*, many have betrayed themselves, and the best principles, by looks or words that have declared an inward shame of religion; and by yielding to the abuse of it, rather than standing up for the honour and importance of the divine commands."[15]

Some Preachers recognized that style and tone matter when talking to adolescents. Teaching about the fear of God to a demographic that places a high value on "fearless and adventurous behavior" was thought likely to backfire and "to cast a gloom over the mind, and to spoil the liberties and pleasures to which young people give up themselves."[16] Better to focus on God's love, goodness, blessings, and promises of a full life, not as an alternative to a deeply devout life but rather as the foundation for it.

From *A Friendly Admonition to Youth to Avoid Bad Company*

Let me remind you, that, by giving up yourselves to sensuality, you efface all serious impressions from your mind. You reflect disgrace and scandal on your religion. You forfeit the favour of your Almighty Maker. You ruin your fortune, your health, your reputation: You make yourselves pests to society. You give offence to virtuous and good men; and become stumbling-blocks to the weak and the unwary. What inexpressible anguish also must you occasion your unhappy parents, to see you thus swerving from the right way: To see you disgracing them by your useless and immoral lives: to see you thus repaying, basely repaying, all their tenderness, all their affectionate hopes, their anxious thoughts, their alarming fears, their painful concern for your welfare. Ungrateful creatures! Is this a proper return to make them; to be a sword in their bowels, and to pierce them through with many sorrows?

~ Joseph Robertson (1784, p. 9)

At the same time, it was considered important to uphold standards, expectations, and boundaries for adolescents. Older adults who "think it a mighty kindness to young people, to excuse even profaneness, and immoralities" were called out for such careless interaction.[17] The antidote to hellfire and brimstone was not hands-off detachment but rather intentional, thoughtful, and honest interaction—which of course wasn't always welcomed by the younger generation. In the words of one preacher when comparing the faith of his adolescent congregants to the faith of Josiah (who "in addition to temptations common to young people, had to struggle with the disadvantages of a bad education—a corrupt court—an idolatrous nation, but who, notwithstanding, *while he was yet young,* at only sixteen years of age, *began to seek after the God of David his father"*): "Much as I love and respect you, my young friends, I must not flatter you."[18]

And so he, like many Preachers before and after him, hammered home the truth about sin (over and over and over again) but then moved on to a long discussion of conversion, faith, service, obedience, joy and love. In other words, adolescents were not just publically called away from a life of selfish sin; they were also called towards a life of genuine devotion. For all of their negative naysaying, Preachers believed a life of genuine devotion was in fact possible for adolescents.

This is stunningly significant: Those adults who were the most vocal about the sins, weaknesses, and failings of adolescents were also the most hopeful about the potential of those adolescents to experience true and lasting inner transformation, not just modified outward behavior.

How was that to happen, though? Parents were continually upheld as the most important spiritual influence on their children's lives (and also as the ones most hurt and disappointed when their adolescent children's religious principles were shaken and religious practices were corrupted by the "bewitching charms of false pleasure").[19] But Preachers also recognized their own role in the lives of adolescents and knew that it was not always as effective as it ought to be. Preaching in 1716, William Bartlet said:

> There is nothing a true minister has more at heart than the success of the ever-blessed gospel, and the enlargement of Christ's Kingdom. This is the main end of his office and ministry. For this a minister lives, speaks, and acts. This is his present joy, and future crown. He does not enter into the Church's service to eat

her bread, and bear an honourable character within her, but to work and labour for the conversion of souls.[20]

Barlet's vision for ministry was clear.

So was his assessment of Christendom and clergy. Even back then—300 years ago, when many of us assume all was well in the Church, in society, and in families—there was unrest and worry. In Bartlet's view, the Church was not experiencing true conversion in her congregants, and he believed this was due in large part to the preachers of the gospel. Along with a litany of other problems, he points specifically to the Church's strategy and practice regarding adolescents.

> Another great defect in our management, and which very much obstructs the success of the gospel, seems to be a want of taking a due care of the youth of our congregations … if we have any prospect of success at all, it lies chiefly among the young generation … Preaching does very little good where catechizing is wholly laid aside. The one prepares for the other … but here perhaps we are as defective in our management of this part of our work as any. 'Tis not the teaching of children that is here principally intended but the instructing the grown and more advanced youth: and here again, not so much the teaching them a set of phrases as the making them understand the true grounds of religion.[21]

The "grown and more advanced youth"—i.e., the adolescents— were on Bartlet's radar, even before radar was a thing. If his language and style were updated for today, his message would ring just as true now as one hopes it did 300 years ago. Preachers often expressed the importance of nurturing a deep faith in their adolescent-aged congregants. They tied deep faith to sincere and heartfelt conversion, often using Jesus' parable of the Lost Son as a biblical model. "The prodigal son came first to himself by consideration, and then he came home to his father by sound conversion … O would but young men retire from the noise and foolish vanities of this world, and allow their souls leisure for the serious exercise of this important duty"[22]—i.e., considering their sinful ways and embracing true conversion. Preachers warned about shallow faith in those whose "juvenile extravagancies" were never fully surrendered and transformed, resulting in a whole population of young people who "almost are half-Christians"—or in twenty-first-century lingo are "almost Christian." They were not a 1700s version of today's *nones*.[23] They were perhaps closer to being "spiritual but not religious."

From *Great Duty and Necessity of a [Virtuous] and Religious Education of Youth: A Sermon*
[If youth are] never shewn the grounds and the reasons of the Christian religion, when he can give no manner of reason why he believes the Bible rather than the Talmud or the Alcoran [Koran], nor why he is a Christian rather than a Jew or a Turk, but only this, that Christianity was the religion of his country and descended to him from his parents; is not such a one left open and defenseless to atheism and to infidelity, to be of any or of no religion as temptations fall in his way. Must not that faith in God and that belief in Christ stand upon a very weak and tottering foundation, which has no solid reason or instruction, but only mere fate and prejudice to support and maintain it?

~ Martin Strong (1707, p. 10)

Some Preachers clearly articulated the differences and importance of both religion *and* relationship, a distinction that is widely appealed to today. "God will have no respect at all to any service that you offer up to him, as long as you with-hold your hearts from him … For this, as has been hinted, is the *foundation* of all religious practice … For while *this* is neglected, the doing of other things will be to no purpose."[24] Youth were encouraged not just to attend Sunday services but to live a life of obedience all week long because God is "not only their father's God, but their God also."[25] If they learned to worship faithfully now, not because they had to but because they wanted to—because "God has given rational souls to you that you might understandingly praise the Lord"—then it was believed they would continue in the faith and fulfill their spiritual purpose: to glorify God.[26]

Some Preachers anticipated the possible objections of adolescents to such a high calling.

Objection one: "It is not the manner of young men and maids to serve and glorify God." Rather they prefer to "do as others do" (i.e., follow the crowd).[27] The Preacher's response: If Samuel, David, Solomon, and Josiah could do it, so can you.

Objection two: "Now is our only time to enjoy our pleasures." The Preacher's response: It's no loss to not enjoy pleasures of sin—besides, a life of obedience also offers pleasures, even better pleasures. In other words, Preachers told adolescents they were saved *to* something and *for* something, not just *from* something.

Objection three: "It is not to be expected that we should be as good as elder people: We are not guilty of any great extravagances: You would not have us to be as religious and as precise as elderly persons." The Preacher's response: Of course we do. In fact, you can be better than some older people. Salvation is not shallow and lukewarm and loose. It is wondrous. And it can be yours just as much as your parents or any other adult.

Really? Did Preachers-of-old really truly believe that adolescents—who were known to engage in a litany of dreadful, deadly, and debauched behaviors—could have a real, sincere, genuine, and lasting life of faith?

Well, yes in fact they did.

> **From *The Obligations to Mental Improvement Stated, and the Use of Books Recommended, Especially to Youth: A Sermon***
> During that period which may be denominated youth, as distinguished from infancy and childhood, I particularly recommend attention to their reading ... Young people are more especially exposed to the temptations of wasting time in unprofitable pursuits and idleness. How many hours, in these last six weeks, has many a careless youth spent in idle exercises, which, had they been employed in reading, would have turned to good account.
>
> ~ George Whitfield (1792, p. 5, 26)

Even without the benefit of national studies and surveys, the Preachers were well aware of the draw of an unchurched life, the lure of atheism, and the temptation of I'll-get-around-to-it-later religiosity, especially for those in adolescence and young adulthood—those who had moved beyond fully controlled and monitored childhood but not yet moved into fully independent and established adulthood. They knew about it. They warned about it. They spoke, wrote, and rallied against it. And then they trusted, hoped, believed, and labored towards a different narrative for the youth in their congregations, parishes, villages, and neighborhoods.

That's what Preachers do—the Preachers who see and love

adolescents, at least—because they know that youth is the best time of life to encourage and nurture a person's present spiritual identity and eternal spiritual self. Even without a midweek youth group, a Sunday morning youth service, a weeknight small group, and a full array of youth events, camps, retreats, and service projects, Preachers have had their eyes on adolescents, not primarily to catch them in the act of screwing up their lives (though they did sometimes do that) but rather to stay connected to them in whatever way possible. It's probably safe to assume that they both failed and succeeded at this way-back-when as much as we do today. But it is *not* safe to assume that only in the past century have adolescents been in the Church's sights. Not by a long shot. No matter what anyone says.

ENDNOTES

1. What better place to note that the sermon quotes inserted throughout this chapter do not represent the whole of Preachers' words and beliefs about *adolescentce*. They are mere snippets and glimpses of larger texts. These lean heavily towards the negative side. Rest assured, the complete sermons include plenty of positive rhetoric and extensive lists of how to counteract sin and nurture strong spiritual formation. These snippets are intended to simply give a small taste of just one aspect of the Preachers' words.

2. Early English Books Online, years 1475-1700; Eighteenth Century Collections Online, years 1700-1800; Early American Imprints, years 1639-1800.

3. I read carefully for specific phrases or definitions that clearly indicate the author/preacher is talking about 1) those at or past puberty or the age of discretion, and 2) those still at least partially under the control or supervision of adults.

4. Thomas Adams, *The Blacke Devill or the Apostate Together with The Wolfe Worrying the Lambes and The Spiritual Navigator Bound for the Holy Land.* (London: Printed by William Jaggard, 1615), 58.

5. Ibid., 58.

6. Samuel Pomfret. *A Directory for Youth Through All the Difficulties Attending that State of Life. Or a Discourse of Youthful Lusts in Which the Nature and Kinds of Them Are Described, and Remedies Against Them Laid Down. First Preached to Young People, and Now Published at Their Request.* (London: Printed for John Dunton at the Black-Raven in the Poultry, 1693), 49.

7. *Two Sermons Preached by the Boy Bishop*, John Gough Nichols, ed., in Volume 7 of *The Camden Miscellany* (London: Camden Society, 1875), 10.

8. Ibid., 10.

9. Pomfret, 52.

10. Henry Burton, *A Divine Tragedie Lately Acted, or A Collection of Sundry memorable examples of God's judgments upon Sabbath-breakers, and other like Libertines, in their unlawfull sports* (1636), 31.

11. Ibid., 33. The Latin word *maleferiati* can be translated an "ill-timed holiday," and in this case it is more specifically referring to an "inappropriate use of the holy day."

12. John B. Romeyn, *The Danger and Duty of Young People: a Sermon Delivered in the Presbyterian Church, in Cedar-Street, New York, April 1, 1810.* (New York: Williams and Whiting, 1810), 20.

13. Solomon Stoddard, *Three Sermons Lately Preach'd at Boston [...] to which a fourth is added, To Stir up Young Men and Maidens to Praise the Name of the* LORD. (Boston: 1717), 105-106.

14. Pomfret, 7-9.

15. Samuel Wright, *The Occasional Preacher No. V: Of Early Piety or the Fear of God in the Days of Youth*, (London: printed and sold by J. Bettenham and J. Roberts, 1741), 16-17.

16. Ibid., 10.

17. Ibid., 23.

18. John Stephens, *Youth Exhorted to Seek God: A Sermon, Delivered in the Methodist Chapel, Canterbury, April the 30th*, 1799, NP. (1799), 3-4, 7.

19. Joseph Robertson, *A Friendly Admonition to Youth to Avoid Bad Company: A Sermon Preached at St. John's Chapel in Sleights.* (York: Printed by A. Ward, 1784), 9-11.

20. William Bartlet, *Barnabas's Character and Success: A Sermon Preach'd at Exon, May the 9th*, 1716. (London: Printed for John Clark at the Bible and Crown in the Poultry, near Cheapside, 1716), 3.

21. Bartlet, 32-33.

22. Pomfret, 81.

23. The term *none* comes from Pew Research's 2014 Religious Landscape Study that has been widely discussed recently. For more detailed information, see: http://www.pewforum.org/2015/05/12/americas-changing-religious-landscape/.

24. John Greene, *A New-Years-Gift to Youth: A Sermon Preach'd at Leicester, January the 1st, 1713. To Young Persons.* (London: Printed by P. Gwillim in Austin-Fryars, for John Clarke at the Bible and Crown in the Old-Change, 1713), 13.

25. Solomon Stoddard, *Three Sermons Lately Preach'd at Boston [...] to which a fourth is added, To stir up Young Men and Maidens to Praise the Name of the* LORD. (Boston: 1717), 98.

26. Ibid., 113.

27. Ibid., 117.

IN SEARCH OF ADOLESCENTS | V

Thinkers, Creators, and Preachers throughout recorded history have said many things about *adolescentce*. So have lots of other people not discussed in this book, including policy-makers, parents, and educators. Most of what this book has examined are verbal and visual representations and descriptions of *adolescentce*, which are not necessarily an accurate reflection of actual adolescent experiences. Still, we have to start somewhere, and those representations and descriptions do provide concrete information about (no surprise here) how (some) Thinkers, Creators, and Preachers presented and described *adolescentce* throughout the centuries. Some of what's been said in the historical past is encouraging. Some is complementary. Some is pejorative. Some is outrageous. Some is ridiculous. Some is hopeful. Some is entertaining. Some is thought-provoking. Some is plain old provoking. Much like the things said, sung, and written about *adolescentce* today, the historical saying, singing, and writing covered the gamut.

The real question for us is: *So what?*

So what if Thinkers, Creators, and Preachers (and policy-makers, parents, and educators) have recognized and pontificated about *adolescentce* for hundreds of years? So what if adolescence isn't a new idea and adolescents aren't a new demographic? So what if adolescence isn't a recent social construct? So what if adolescents aren't simply modern-day high school students? So what if the historical realities aren't what we imagined them to be? So what if humanity has long recognized and described an in-between stage of life, bridging childhood and adulthood? So what if adults' descriptions of *adolescentce*—both good and bad—are surprisingly consistent throughout the past millenium?

Does that really matter today for those who work with adolescents, mentor adolescents, teach adolescents, and parent adolescents? Or for those who study adolescence, research adolescence, theorize about adolescence, and teach about adolescence? Are our actions, words, and thoughts affected or shaped in any way by the popular historical narrative such that a revised historical narrative would have an obvious and visible impact?

On a daily practical level, I rather doubt it.

When planning youth group events or outlining a small group lesson, I suspect most youth workers do not think to themselves, "I must remember that my youth are the product of a socially constructed life stage that has only existed for about a hundred years. Ergo, we will employ only the most modern strategies. Dodgeball it is." (Assuming, of course, people have only been chucking balls at each other for the past century, which is pretty doubtful.)

When navigating a challenging season alongside one's own teenager, I suspect most parents do not think, "Deep breath in. Deep breath out. Remember: They're navigating a life stage that isn't natural or normal, so I must do my best to use only non-conventional—rather than natural or logical—response tactics. Dodgeball it is."

That's what I suspect, anyway, based on many years of youth ministry involvement and many years of raising three adolescents of my own. I don't think that a course-corrected historical framework is likely to change our most basic day-to-day practical decisions and actions.

But that doesn't mean a course-corrected historical framework doesn't matter. I think it matters quite a lot, for several reasons.

First, in our ever-speedier and ever-broader information-ingesting age—in which we draw ever closer to the omniscience and omnipresence we've coveted since Day One—we risk becoming less and less aware of and connected to a real (versus an imagined) past. We risk becoming not just people who forget, but people who never knew in the first place.

Though we look ahead with good reason, we forego looking back at our own peril. If and when we finally do look back, it is often with a preconceived idea about what we'll find, or it is with rose-tinted glasses that foolishly and blindly project a picture of bliss, joy, and goodness, as though the current human condition is a direct result of smartphones and air-conditioning rather than a direct result of being human.

From the get-go, humanity has been a mess, albeit a mess that embodies stunning degrees of God's beauty, joy, and blessedness. History only confirms the messiness. For some reason, though, our historical portrait of the supposed nonexistence of adolescence has taken on epic proportions. And by proxy, our historical portrait of the growing-up process has become mythically rooted. We envision children passing out of childhood (instantaneously), passing through puberty (easily), and then passing into adulthood (*hey! presto!*) *sans* any of the confusion, questions, troubles, tangles, and angst that seem to have become rampantly typical and emotionally crippling for every single adolescent, at least in the popular narrative. We envision our grandparents and their grandparents before them living in some kind of utopic coming-of-age universe that had no attendant issues surrounding identity development, transitioning away from parental authority, or finding one's place in the world. Apparently, that all worked itself out quickly and happily for most of history.

It's easy to see how a person might become disgruntled at the severe turn things have taken in the last century. If only we (and the adolescents, of course—let's not forget them) could return to those good old days of no-adolescence. In a perfect world, we would dial back a few centuries to live blissful lives—and we would bring our smartphones and air-conditioning with us.

But identity development, the pull away from parental authority, disappointments, making difficult decisions, and finding one's place in the world *are not new issues*. They look different in the twenty-first century than they did in the twentieth century, the nineteenth century, and every century before that. But they are not new. Seventeenth-century parents agonized over what apprenticeship would best suit their adolescent sons and daughters, and then agonized over whether they had the means and opportunity to attain them. Sixteenth-century university educators wrung their hands in despair over their inability to control their students' outrageous behaviors. Fifteenth-century adolescents fought with their parents about how they spent their leisure time. Fourteenth-century adolescents fell into depths of depression and despair when their romantic relationships failed or were prohibited. Thirteenth-century adolescents struggled against restraints on their limited freedoms. In every century, adolescents have been handed a mixed bag of adult rights and responsibilities on the one hand and adolescent restraints and limitations on the other. The contexts were notably different. The degree and manner of the experiences were vastly different. But the contexts and the experiences were just as real to those in other centuries as ours are to us today.

This does have some serious implications for those people who use erroneous history to claim that adolescents should be emancipated at a younger age and given full adult rights and responsibilities at that time.[1] An amended historical record would seriously deflate their arguments and claims.

Still, on a solely practical level—*how should I program Wednesday night? how should I respond to my boundary-pushing adolescent?*—I hesitate to offer any solid and immediate implications of a revised historical narrative. So far, that is.

But on various theoretical and theological levels, we should begin to think about some things that may eventually lead to more practical discussions. I say this based on several conversations I've had in the last few years.

Two of those conversations happened when I presented the very cursory twelve-minute mash-up of the history of adolescence I mentioned earlier.[2] After a lengthy follow-up discussion forum, a college student waited patiently for the room to clear so we could speak in private. She was focused, intent, and articulate.

"I'm mortified," she said. Mortified? That was a new one. People had told me they were surprised, or skeptical, or wholly disbelieving about my historical research, but never mortified. "I'm a Classics major. I've been taught to think for myself, to never accept a blanket statement as fact without personally confirming it, to do my research. I believed that adolescence is a recent social construct because that's what someone told me and taught me in one of my classes. I never questioned it. I didn't ask how we know this is true. I never looked for supporting evidence. I never did my own fact-checking. *I am mortified at my own academic laziness.*"

She was serious, to the point of being somewhat agitated. This obviously mattered to her.

I realized then that historical accuracy regarding *adolescentce* has deeper implications than simply, "Hey—we might want to reconsider the framework upon which we've built some of our suppositions about adolescence, culture, and youth ministry." It also speaks to issues of pedagogy, authority, foundational principals, and intellectual responsibility.

A short time later, I was approached by a small group of middle-aged youth workers. They had skipped the follow-up discussion forum because they wanted some time and space to process the historical mash-up among themselves. Unlike the college student, who was intellectually upended, these adults were emotionally rattled. A few had clearly been crying. At least one was still teary. She spoke passionately.

"I'm *so very relieved*," she said. Relieved? This was a new one. People had told me they were ambivalent, or only slightly curious, or maybe perhaps a bit fascinated, but never relieved. "Besides being a youth worker, I have my own teenagers. I've been told—and I've believed—that adolescence is not natural because it's a social construct. If it's not the way things are supposed to be, then what hope is there for parents? I have been worried, stressed, and fearful wondering what chance there was for raising healthy and whole teenagers. I've sometimes felt like things were futile, that if only we could go back in time, before adolescence existed, things would be better. The fact that this stage of life isn't new and that parents have been trying to understand it and deal with it positively throughout history is so encouraging to me."

She hugged me. Really.

I realized then that the historical accuracy regarding adolescence has deeper implications than simply, "Hey—we might want to reconsider the framework upon which we've built some of our suppositions about adolescence, culture, and youth ministry." It also speaks to issues of parenting, mentoring, family structures, and spiritual encouragement.

But *how* exactly does it speak to these larger issues? And why does that matter? And what should we do about it?

QUESTIONS FOR TODAY

Those are big questions that are going to require the ideas and thoughts of many wise people—academics, practitioners, researchers, pastors, parents, and more. This book lays a foundation on which those conversations can take place. In the meantime, here are some thoughts and questions to consider now.

1. How do we learn and discern? Based on the survey mentioned in Chapter One and numerous personal conversations, one thing is clear: People believe adolescence is a recent social construct because someone or something said so. They were taught this fact, often by well-meaning, intelligent, and intellectual people who do in fact know better than anyone else what they are talking about within their particular field of study. So we are inclined to accept and believe this relatively small detail of their discourse because we know how trustworthy the rest of their information is.

Fair enough.

But how often do we accept similarly presented "facts" from people who are not trustworthy, regardless of their education or intellect? How often do we believe what someone says without ever asking questions, thinking for ourselves, chasing down our own answers, or applying commonsense logic? In this particular context, we have every reason to hope that little to no damage has been done. But in other instances, where a popular narrative has become accepted as fact, and where that narrative has direct implications on how we live, interact, communicate, work, worship, or what have you, there are all kinds of ways things could take a very wrong turn. It's happened countless times throughout history, both in society at large and in the Church. It's the very core of propaganda. Thank goodness this particular issue isn't a propaganda one *per se*, though in the world of policy-making, our current narrative certainly has the potential to shape laws and practices in ways that perhaps are neither wise nor warranted.

We bestow significant authority on written texts—books in some cases, the Internet in others (and let's not even get started on all those "best quotes" websites that almost never provide a source title, let alone a specific page number, and which more times than not are either falsely attributed or erroneously quoted, and which many speakers, authors, teachers, and pastors find especially delightful and useful; or all of those reposts on social media that are eventually exposed as flat out false but only after 10,000 people have liked and reposted them: I digress). Perhaps it is not surprising that such authority has been bestowed on books ever since the written word appeared. "It is written" is not just a scriptural appeal. It was an academic appeal in the Middle Ages, where the "auctoritee" of books was broadly upheld. Spreading "facts" has become shockingly easy and quick in the information age. Checking those facts isn't quite as easy or quick; but it is entirely possible and eminently responsible to do just that.

A further consideration is this: While we must necessarily learn some things via an intermediary—teacher, coach, mentor, parent, etc.—we must never learn this way exclusively. C. S. Lewis hinted at this in his Introduction to *The Incarnation of the Word of God* where he encourages people to read old books partly as a way to directly acquire ideas, thoughts, information, and truth.[3] Rather than reading *about* Plato, St. Matthew, or Augustine, he says, read Plato, St. Matthew, or Augustine themselves. In Lewis's opinion, it is almost always easier to understand the direct source than someone else's exposition and analysis of it. Rather than accepting someone's mediated facts and ideas, research and read them personally—when time and opportunity allow, which admittedly isn't always. Still, it is good practice for all of us to confirm for ourselves the veracity of "It is written" as often as possible.

2. How do we view the past and why? We often do with the past what many do with *adolescentce*: either romanticize it as a nearly perfect pristine slice of time or vilify it as an unenlightened barbarian swamp of grotesque ills. No doubt someone has theorized about why we do this and has conducted various studies to prove their theories. Here are my two cents' worth: We (sometimes) either romanticize or vilify the past because we (often) do not like dealing with reality. It is too complicated, too messy, too fussy, too unpredictable, too confusing, and all other kinds of "too." We are happier when everything is either colored inside the lines with a basic and pleasing palette or scribbled in the margins with disturbing and opposing hues. Our responses and actions don't require as much forethought or nuance when things are either A or B. It is much easier to say, "Back then, everyone _____" or "Back then no one _____" or "Back then everything _____" or "Back then nothing _____," than it is to try and detangle all the different threads of culture, religion, society, people, more people, and also some more people.

It's a bit (just a very little bit, perhaps) like some of the New Testament conversations.

> Pharisees: *We say A, others say B, what do you say?*
> Jesus: *I say seven.*

It's not just a matter of balancing A and B. It's a matter of thinking on an entirely different plane. In this case, the reality is not one of two blanket statements, "adolescence is new" or "adolescence has been exactly the same for hundreds of years." Rather, it is a search: "What were people saying about adolescence 200 years ago? And 300 years ago? And 400 years ago? And before that?" because without doubt they *were* saying things. The search for, "What was the adolescent experience like 200 years ago? And 300 years ago? And 400 years ago? And before that?" is more challenging because the voices of adolescents have never been turned "up to 11" and because the adolescent experience 200, 300, 400, and more years ago was as widely varied between communities, ethnicities, social classes, and genders as it is today. But the extant sources can tell us quite a lot about the actual adolescent experience, which is the focus of my ongoing search.

I believe the past matters, and though we cannot all spend our time muddling through old this-and-thats, some people should.

In his inaugural address at Cambridge, later adapted for the radio, C. S. Lewis said this to the student body regarding the study of medieval and renaissance literature:

> I do not think you need fear that the study of a dead period, however prolonged and however sympathetic, need prove an indulgence in nostalgia or an enslavement to the past. In the individual life, as the psychologists have taught us, it is not the remembered but the forgotten past that enslaves us. I think the same is true of society. To study the past does indeed liberate us from the present, from the idols of our own market-place. But I think it liberates us from the past too. I think no class of men are less enslaved to the past than historians. The unhistorical are usually, without knowing it, enslaved to a fairly recent past.[4]

3. How do we view the present and why? As mentioned earlier, there is a tendency for many people to view the present as both the height of human accomplishment ("we are so very much more intellectual and theologically wise and all-around advanced than those who came before us, thank the good Lord") and the epitome of human struggling ("good Lord, our problems are bigger, our hurts are deeper, our challenges are wider, our cultural battles are bloodier"). We are not the first generation to embrace these extremes. The second has proven to have an extraordinarily long shelf life, especially in the Church. Sermon after sermon in century after century lamented, "Woe unto us who do dwell in this most wicked cesspool of a wasteland filthified beyond words by worldly decadence," or something along those lines, regardless of whether the subject was youth, politics, families, secular music, fashion, or any of countless other things gone bad.

How do you view the present, specifically in terms of the

adolescents you know and minister to? Do you have a sense of woe? Do you find yourself leaning towards despair on their behalf? Does it seem like they are navigating an unfair share of challenges, brokenness, temptations, and misdirection?

Every generation has felt similarly, and while it is tempting for us to look backwards and laugh off the seemingly mild "wicked temptations" of old, for the people involved those "wicked temptations" were very real and represented the height of genuine concern. The dangerous lure of unguarded virtual realties may seem a thousand times worse to us, but I predict that in just a few years, unguarded virtual realities may seem tame when compared to whatever the current cultural tidal wave may be. They certainly don't feel tame to us right now though. So we might be considerate enough to those-of-old to acknowledge and accept the legitimate intensity of their specific worries and fears.

There are two different ways we can credibly respond to this.

> **Way 1:** If the general nature of adult fears, worries, hopes and goals regarding *adolescentce* lean towards consistency throughout history *except in terms of their immediate context, i.e., culture,* then youth workers must absolutely be up-to-date and intimately familiar with said culture in order to have an effective ministry.

> **Way 2:** If the general nature of adult fears, worries, hopes and goals regarding *adolescentce* lean towards consistency throughout history *regardless of their immediate context, i.e., culture,* then youth workers need not be thoroughly up-to-date and intimately familiar with said culture in order to have an effective ministry.

A solid case can be made for both of these views *except in their most extreme forms* wherein a youth worker is more aware of adolescent culture than adolescents or a youth worker is so entirely unaware of adolescent culture that he or she cannot possibly be fully aware of adolescents.

There are countless things to lament in every generation—ours included. There are infinite reasons to be hopeful in every generation—ours included. Present culture most certainly informs and shapes our ministries, *but it does not define them.* If that were to ever happen, culture will have won and we will likely be unaware of its victory.

4. How do we view *adolescentce*? We may have come a long way in understanding adolescent neurology, adolescent psychology, and various other adolescentologies, but everyday thinking about *adolescentce* often tends to embrace the two extremes so prevalent throughout history: We either romanticize and idealize both the stage of life and those in it, or we negatively stereotype—sometimes to the point of demonizing—the age and its players.

If an adolescent hits the headlines, it is usually either because they have done, said, or accomplished something stupendous (running for city government at age seventeen; graduating from an Ivy League school at age sixteen; inventing a new medical device at age fifteen; starting a ministry to help free developing-world sex slaves at age fourteen) or because they have done, said, or been found guilty of something unthinkable (shooting classmates and teachers; torching a mall in Baltimore; going on a four-state crime spree; murdering their grandparents). We pay attention to the really good and the really bad. Their faces, names, and stories infiltrate both the real and the virtual world. The first are upheld as the superlative model to be copied; the second are condemned as evil, raising fears of what may lie within other adolescents.

The "really good" and the "really bad" adolescents—whether real or fictive—receive a lion's share of the attention, while a lion's share of adolescents do not fit into either of those parameters. They are the in-betweens (the neither-saintly-good-nor-devilishly-bad) of the in-betweens (the no-longer-a-kid-not-yet-an-adult). They are a much less flashy and star-studded, typically human combination of good and bad, strengths and weaknesses, talents and shortcomings, ups and downs. But that is precisely who we must be noticing—the unlikely-to-be-noticed—because they are, in fact, star-studded beyond words:

> When I look at the night sky and see the work of your
>   fingers—
>   the moon and the stars you set in place—
> What are mere adolescent mortals that you should think
>   about them,
>   teenaged human beings that you should care for them?
> Yet you made them only a little lower than the angels
>   and crowned them with glory and honor.
>
>   – Psalm 8 (NLT, amplified a tiny bit)

The middle is a hard place to be, especially if being in the middle also feels ordinary, unspectacular, unstupendous, and unnoticed—rather like Chaucer's Squire who was neither very good nor very bad but just … average … which is to say, just breathtaking.

5. How do we view youth ministry? Indeed. How *do* we view youth ministry, and by extension youth ministers? And by youth ministers I mean every single Christ-following adult who ever has, ever does, and ever will come in contact with an adolescent. *We are all youth ministers, because we are all ministers of the gospel and we all know at least one youth.*

Are we then primarily educators? Shapers? Molders?

Guardians? Entertainers? Counselors? Disciplers?
Disciplinarians? Greeters? Evangelists? Encouragers?
Catechists? Programmers? Chaperones? Parent figures? Pals?
Protectors? Sounding posts?

Probably. Yes. Those things. Some hopefully much, much less
than others. And by "much, much less" I mean hardly at all.

Full-time remunerated vocational youth ministry, like many
other church staff roles, is not a centuries-old career. But
youth ministry—seeing adolescents, caring for adolescents,
spiritually nurturing adolescents, teaching adolescents, training
adolescents, mentoring adolescents, catechizing adolescents,
discipling adolescents, correcting adolescents, challenging
adolescents, and most importantly knowing adolescents—has
been going on for a very long time, probably for as long as there
have been adolescents.[5] Consider the book of Proverbs. Or the
grooming of Daniel and the other adolescent-aged Israelites, a
prime example of what youth ministry must never be.

For centuries, Preachers have recognized the importance
of ministering to youth. Today's youth workers and youth
ministers may be treading new ground in terms of content,
programming, scheduling, and style. *But they are not treading
brand new ground.* They are this generation's link in a long
chain of people who have pursued adolescents. We are not the
first to notice them, cry for them, pray for them, care for them,
and love them. There is a long legacy before us, albeit one that
has taken many different shapes, styles, twists, and turns.

Youth ministers of all shape and manner are today standing on the
shoulders of faithful followers of Christ from every previous era,
and a new generation of youth ministers will someday be standing
on our shoulders. *Our shoulders*—which are really just the hands
and feet of Jesus. But still. It's quite astounding to consider.

CHALLENGES FOR THE ROAD AHEAD

And finally, in an attempt to start pulling these various threads together and to inject at least a bit of immediate practical direction, four challenges.

1. We must not live or minister in an insular bubble, whether of context or chronology. If we read only youth ministry books that present practical ways to do X, Y, and Z, we are engaging in a very limited conversation. We can and should learn from other people, other disciplines, other angles, and other contexts. And if we read only new books that present important ideas about just up-to-the-minute issues, we run the risk of seeing those issues as singularly definitive. That is, we risk knowing about nothing beyond the walls of youth ministry, and we risk placing onto all our adolescents certain emotions, behaviors, tendencies, sorrows, struggles, or identities, whether or not they are actually present in their lives.

Read the youth ministry books. Read the new books. Absolutely. Learn all you can from the people who gather, analyze, sort, think about, and study *adolescentce*. Listen to what they say. Consider carefully the premises, the theories, and the conclusions. Expand and hone your youth ministry mentality and practices. Live into your calling and passion.

But please, *read Scripture more than you read anything else, and read your own individual youth more than you read about youth in general.* Go straight to the primary source. Study it. Read it. Read it again. Read it over and over and over. Spend time with it. Listen to it. Enjoy it. Learn from it. Engage with it. And by "it," of course, I mean her. I mean him. I mean them.

In our reading, learning, and studying, we honor our ministry calling by engaging in a purposed search for **adolescence**. In our ministry with youth, we honor our identity as followers of Christ by engaging in a purposed search for **adolescents**. The main focus of those who spend time with adolescents in whatever capacity must always be adolescents themselves, living in the here and now, dealing with the nitty-gritty, as they are being and becoming the individual God created, envisioned, intended, and breathed the breath of life into.

2. We must be careful not to construct larger narratives around smaller narratives for which we have no concretely solid support. Over the years, we have taken a small narrative (i.e., adolescence is a recent invention of the modern world resulting from specific social changes) and have erected a much larger narrative around it (i.e., adolescents are trying to navigate an unnatural stage of life; adolescents are being locked out of adulthood and therefore are acting out in dangerous ways; adolescents have all the capacities and faculties of adults, if we would only set them free from all counsel and constraints; adolescents are extending their adolescence into what should be adulthood because society has made it so difficult for them to grow up fully; as adolescence has taken hold, the maturity they displayed in previous generations has been lost to the wind; adolescents are being robbed of their natural right to exercise total autonomy; and more).

Exactly what steps were involved in how these larger narrative details grew out of the smaller narrative is up for debate. But it isn't difficult to imagine how it might have happened. They all sound logical and seem to make sense—*if the smaller narrative is actually true.* After a while, the larger narrative becomes so accepted that the significance of the smaller narrative is lost or forgotten and we have successfully closed the door to any historical inquiry or consideration.

In our world of oversaturated information flying at us from

every direction at breakneck speed, we stand poised to grasp whatever narrative slice might grab our attention and to then build a larger narrative around it that may not be entirely—or even remotely—accurate. Snarky skepticism has been known to destroy some people's ability to enjoy anything in life. But healthy skepticism is not a bad thing when directed at theories, generalizations, and intellectual narratives. This is not to imply that there are endless holes to be poked in our collective wealth of knowledge. It is simply to say that querying, wondering, pondering, and even debating (ever so politely, and only when warranted) are okay. Perhaps more than okay. Perhaps important and necessary. Perhaps indeed.

3. We must be open, grateful, gracious, and welcoming to any and all faithful and truthful youth ministers. Though Preachers-of-old—the main head honcho guys of the Church— did much of the religious instructing and spiritual nurturing of youth within the church walls, those same Preachers made impassioned appeals to any number of adults to do the same outside of the church walls: parents (first and foremost), magistrates, teachers, apprenticeship masters, and more. They did not worry about guarding their turf or protecting their ownership of specific souls.[6]

If we are serious about searching for adolescents in the most intentional and spiritual sense, then we should not be cataloguing "our" kids or building fences around "our" ministries or privatizing "our" programs. None of us can lay claim to any of those things—least of all an individual soul.

Instead, we should joyfully and happily link arms with every person and entity who follows and preaches Christ crucified and risen and who is passionate and committed to the spiritual growth, nurture, and discipleship of an adolescent. That might be the youth pastor at a church across town. That might be an adult who isn't officially involved in the youth ministry. That might be a Bible study that meets in the public high school, led by a teacher who doesn't attend your church. That might be a parachurch ministry that focuses primarily on evangelism, or one that encourages discipleship, or one that targets a very specific demographic. If they love Jesus, live Jesus, reflect Jesus, and follow Jesus, more power to them and their ministry— and to you, and to the entire Kingdom. Remember what the real mission is: adolescents + Jesus + discipleship, resulting in genuine and rooted faith. Let's not engage in Apollos versus Paul scorekeeping, us versus them gamesmanship or my church versus your parachurch closed-fistedness. There are much more important things to do—like follow Christ and search for adolescents. And by searching I mostly mean seeing, meeting, knowing, and loving the adolescents already present in our lives and communities who we haven't yet fully seen, met, known, and loved.

4. Our churches must be a place where we intentionally and expertly allow adolescents to celebrate and enjoy what remains of childhood even as we provide intentional and significant opportunities for them to transition into adulthood. To skip either of these would be to minister to only a portion of our adolescents' souls and selves. There continues to be much debate about what this balance should look like—50/50? 60/40? 70/30? Mathematical percentages seem unhelpful. We cannot neatly split an adolescent's identity into its various stages of growing up. But in our ministries, it seems logical to play in ways that invite and celebrate The Child, and to teach in ways that invite and encourage The Adult. In the Church perhaps more than any other context, adolescents should be allowed to have fun that breaks all bounds of what the world considers fun, both in its creativity and its intensity. In the Church perhaps more than any other context, adolescents should be challenged to learn broadly, think critically, and serve meaningfully in ways that break all bounds of what the world considers significant, both in style and depth.

"JUST THE RIGHT TIME"

Fact: Adolescence has been a recognized stage of life—biologically, socially, culturally, and relationally—for a very, very long time. I would argue that in its essence, it is a natural stage of life, one that is specifically and intentionally created by God. He could just as easily have designed the human race to propagate itself in a fully mature state. Or to pass through the various developmental stages quickly, like most of the animal kingdom does.

But that's not what he did. He gave us infants, which is obviously for the parents' benefit since the infants themselves remember nothing of that season. Nor do schoolchildren remember much of childhood. It isn't until adolescence that both the child and the parents (and other adults) are filing away endless memories of the process, a process that too often is belittled and bemoaned. In the context of parenting, Eugene Peterson speaks of this beautifully when he writes:

> The infant is a gift of God by which we are given renewed access to the forms of childlikeness through which we receive our Lord and enter the kingdom of God.

> But the adolescent, though not so obviously, is no less a gift of God. As the infant is God's gift to the young adult, so the adolescent is a gift to the middle-aged. The adolescent is "born" into our lives during our middle decades (when we are in our thirties, forties, and fifties). In these middle decades of life we are prone to stagnation and depression—the wonders of life reduce

to banalities and the juices of life dry up. For many there is a feeling of letdown. The surging strength of early adulthood has not carried us to eminence. Failures and disappointments accumulate. Even when there is outward success, there is often a corresponding inner dryness, a sensation of hollowness, a shriveling of hope. The ideals and expectations of earlier years are experienced as fatigue ...

And then God's gift: in the rather awkward packaging of the adolescent God brings into our lives a challenge to grow, testing our love, chastening our hope, pushing our faith to the edge of the abyss. *It comes at just the right time.*[7] (italics added)

Indeed it does come at just the right time for parents. For youth workers—*joy! surprise! wonder!*—"just the right time" extends far longer than the standard duration. It lasts for as long as we embrace and engage with adolescents.

Humanity is created in the image of God. Ergo, adolescents have much to teach us and show us about his character. They, no less than breathtaking infants, precious children, and settled adults, reflect God's image in unique and profound ways. If we do not search for them, see them, and know them, then we will be the poorer for it because we will have missed out on knowing God in all his fullness. That is as true today as it was 200, 300, 400, and more years ago.

ENDNOTES

1. Robert Epstein is the most vocal promoter of this view, especially in his book *Teen 2.0: Saving Our Children and Families from the Torment of Adolescence* (Quill Driver Books, 2010).
2. The Youth Cartel Summit (Atlanta, GA), November 2013. The talk is available online at http://theyouthcartel.com/summit-presenter/crystal-kirgiss/.
3. C. S. Lewis, Introduction to *The Incarnation of the Word of God* (New York: Macmillan Company, 1946), 5-12. "The simplest student will be able to understand, if not all, yet a very great deal of what Plato said; but hardly anyone can understand some modern books on Platonism. It has always therefore been one of my main endeavours as a teacher to persuade the young that first-hand knowledge is not only more worth acquiring than second-hand knowledge, but usually much easier and more delightful to acquire." (5) Republished as "On the Reading of Old Books" in *God in the Dock* (Grand Rapids, MI: William B. Eerdmans, 1972), 200-207.
4. C. S. Lewis, "The Great Divide" on *C. S. Lewis Speaks His Mind* (Alliance for Christian Media, 2007), compact disc. The program was recorded by the BBC on April 1, 1955, and aired by the same on April 6 and 9, 1955.
5. There has been very little work done on this topic to date, but one example to support this premise can be found in *The Rule of St. Benedict* (Benedict, *The Rule of Saint Benedict*, ed. and trans. Bruce L. Venarde [Cambridge, MA: Harvard University Press, 2011]) where there were different expectations for *adulescentiores fratres* (adolescent brothers) in terms of supervision, instruction, and correction. Regarding the youthful brothers, Benedict writes that "every age and level of intelligence should be treated in its own way" (*Omnis aetas vel intellectus proprias debet habere mansuras*. XXX, 115). Instruction and discipline up to age fifteen must be especially diligent, he said, though it does not end there. Admittedly the religious life is a very specific context and this example cannot be summarily extrapolated. Still, this theoretical practice of interacting with, training, and ministering both to and with youth was real and known.
6. There were plenty of turf wars in the eras of Reformation and Restoration, when Protestant and Catholic spiritual leaders alike were known to fling accusations and judgments like cannonballs, or when certain small sects such as Quakers arose and some non-small sectarians were prone to engage in some serious eyeball stabbing (metaphorically). There has been plenty of not-playing-together-nicely between certain churches throughout the years. I speak here of

something different.
7. Eugene Peterson, *Like Dew Your Youth: Growing Up with Your Teenager* (Eerdmans, [1976] 1994), 3-4.

ADDITIONAL SOURCES

Note: What follows is a select bibliography of relevant sources. Some of the secondary sources in this list recognize a broad and accurate history of adolescence. Others claim that adolescence is a recent cultural construct. Their inclusion in this bibliography is not necessarily a reflection of their historical accuracy, but of the author's research on the subject.

Alexandre-Bidon, Danièle and Didier Lett. *Children in the Middle Ages: Fifth-Fifteenth Centuries*. Translated by Jody Gladding. Notre Dame, IN: University of Notre Dame Press, 1999.

Ausubel, David P. *Theory and Problems of Adolescent Development*. 3rd ed. Lincoln, NE: Writers Club Press, 2002.

Bailey, Meridee L. "In Service and at Home: Didactic Texts for Children and Young People, c. 1400-1600. *Parergon* 24:2 (2007), 23-46.

Beales, Ross W. "In Search of the Historical Child: Miniature Adulthood and Youth in Colonial New England." *American Quarterly* 27 (Oct. 1975): 379-398.

Bell, Rudolph M. *How to Do It: Guides to Good Living for Renaissance Italians.* Chicago: University of Chicago Press, 1999.

Borsay, Peter. "Children, Adolescents and Fashionable Urban Society," In *Fashioning Childhood in the Eighteenth Century: Age and Identity,* ed. Anja Müller. Aldershot: Ashgate Publishing, 2006.

Classen, Albrecht, ed. *Childhood in the Middle Ages and the Renaissance: The Results of a Paradigm Shift in the History of Mentality.* Berlin: Walter de Gruyter, 2005.

Davis, Natalie Zemon. "The Reasons of Misrule." In *Society and Culture in Early Modern France,* 97-123, 296-309. Stanford, CA: Stanford University Press, 1975.

Demos, John and Virginia Demos. "Adolescence in Historical Perspective." *Journal of Marriage and the Family* 31 (1969): 632-38.

Eisenbichler, Kondrad, ed. *The Premodern Teenager: Youth in Society 1150-1650.* Toronto: Centre for Reformation and Renaissance Studies, 2002.

Forsyth, Ilene H. "Children in Early Medieval Art: Ninth Through Twelfth Centuries." *The Journal of Psychohistory* 4 (1976): 31-70.

Fox, Vivian C. "Is Adolescence a Phenomenon of Modern Times?" *Journal of Psychohistory* 5 (1977-1978): 271-90.

Glaser, Brigitte. "Gendered Childhoods: On the Discursive Formation of Young Females in the Eighteenth Century." In *Fashioning Childhood in the Eighteenth Century: Age and Identity.* Edited by Anja Müller, 189-198. Aldershot: Ashgate Publishing, 2006.

Goldberg, P. J. P. and Felicity Riddy, eds. *Youth in the Middle Ages.* Woodbridge: York Medieval Press, 2004.

Graham, Philip. *The End of Adolescence.* Oxford: Oxford University Press, 2004.

Hanawalt, Barbara A. " 'The Childe of Bristowe' and the Making of Middle-Class Adolescence." In *Bodies and Disciplines: Intersections of Literature and History in Fifteenth-Century England.* Edited by Barbara A. Hanawalt and David J. Wallace, 155-78. Minneapolis: University of Minnesota Press, 1996.

———. *Growing Up in Medieval London: The Experience of Childhood in History*. New York: Oxford University Press, 1993.

———. "Historical Descriptions and Prescriptions for Adolescence." *Journal of Family History* 17 (1992): 341-51.

———. *The Ties That Bound: Peasant Families in Medieval England*. New York: Oxford University Press, 1986.

Hiner, N. Ray. "Adolescence in Eighteenth-Century America." *History of Childhood Quarterly* 3 (1975): 253-80.

Johnston, Mark D. *Medieval Conduct Literature: An Anthology of Vernacular Guides to Behaviour for Youths, with English Translations*. Toronto: University of Toronto Press, 2009.

Keniston, Kenneth. "Youth: The 'New' Stage of Life." *The American Scholar* 39 (1970): 631-54.

Kett, Joseph F. "Discovery and Invention in the History of Adolescence." *Journal of Adolescent Health* 14 (1993): 605-12.

———. "Reflections on the History of Adolescence in America." *History of the Family* 8 (2003): 355-73.

Kiell, Norman. *The Universal Experience of Adolescence*. London: University of London Press, 1964.

King, Margaret L. "Concepts of Childhood: What We Know and Where We Might Go." *Renaissance Quarterly* 60 (2007): 371-407.

Klein, Hugh. "Adolescence, Youth, and Young Adulthood: Rethinking Current Conceptualizations of Life Stage." *Youth and Society* 21 (1990): 446-71.

Lesko, Nancy. *Act Your Age! A Cultural Construction of Adolescence*. New York: Routledge, 2001.

Levi, Giovanni and Jean-Claude Schmitt, eds. *A History of Young People in the West: Ancient and Medieval Rites of Passage*. Translated by Camille Naish. Cambridge, MA: Belknap, 1997.

Milis, Ludo. "Children and Youth, The Medieval Viewpoint." *Pedagogica Historica* 29 (1993): 15-32.

Mintz, Steven. "Reflections on Age as a Category of Historical Analysis." *Journal of the History of Childhood and Youth* 1 (2008): 91-94.

Modell, John, and Madeline Goodman. "Historical Perspectives." In *At the Threshold: The Developing Adolescent.* Edited by S. Shirley Feldman and Glen R. Elliott, 93-122. Cambridge, MA: Harvard University Press, 1990.

Nelson, Janet L. "Parents, Children, and the Church in the Earlier Middle Ages (Presidential Address)." *Studies in Church History: Papers Read at the 1993 Summer Meeting and the 1994 Winter Meeting of the Ecclesiastical History Society.* Edited by Diana Wood, 81-114.

Old English Homilies and Homiletic Treatises. Edited with Introduction, Translation, and Notes by Richard Morris. EETS os 29, 34. 1868. Reprint, New York: Greenwood Press, 1969.

Orme, Nicholas. "Children and Literature in Medieval England." *Medium Ævum* 68 (1999): 218-46.

———. *Medieval Children.* New Haven: Yale University Press, 2001.

Owst, G. R. *Literature and Pulpit in Medieval England.* 2nd revised ed. Oxford: Basil Blackwell, 1961.

Reynerson, Kathryn L. "The Adolescent Apprentice/Worker in Medieval Montpellier." *Journal of Family History* 17 (1992): 353-70.

Saltman, Kenneth J. "The Social Construction of Adolescence." In *The Critical Middle School Reader.* Edited by Enora R. Brown and Kenneth J. Saltman, 15-20. New York: Routledge, 2005.

Santrock, John W. *Adolescence.* 11th ed. Boston: McGraw Hill, 2007.

Schlegel, Alice and Herbert Barry III. *Adolescence: An Anthropological Inquiry.* New York: The Free Press, 1991.

Sears, Elizabeth. *The Ages of Man: Medieval Interpretations of the Life Cycle.* Princeton, NJ: Princeton University Press, 1986.

Smith, Steven R. "The London Apprentices as Seventeenth-Century Adolescents." *Past and Present* 62 (Nov. 1973), 149-161.

Steinberg, Laurence and Richard M. Lerner. "The Scientific Study of Adolescence: A Brief History." *The Journal of Early Adolescence* 24:1 (2004): 45-5.

Stoertz, Fiona Harris. "Adolescence in Medieval Culture: The High Medieval Transformation." PhD diss., University of California, Santa Barbara, 1999. UMI (9953932).

———. "Relationships Between Parents and Their Absent Adolescent Offspring in the High Middle Ages." *Medieval Feminist Newsletter* 24 (1997): 38-42.

———. "Sex and the Medieval Adolescent." In *The Premodern Teenager: Youth in Society 1150-1650*. Edited by Konrad Eisenbichler, 225-43. Toronto: Centre for Reformation and Renaissance Studies, 2002.

Thompson, Roger. "Adolescent Culture in Colonial Massachusetts." *Journal of Family History* 9 (1984): 127-44.

Trevisa, John. *On the Properties of Things*. 2 vols. Oxford: Clarendon, 1975.

Violate, Claudio and Arthur J. Wiley. "Images of Adolescence in English Literature: The Middle Ages to the Modern Period." *Adolescence* 25 (1990): 253-64.

Walsham, Alexandra. "The Reformation of the Generations: Youth, Age, and Religious Change in England, c. 1500-1700." *Transaction of the RHS* 21 (2011): 93-121.

Wells, Sharon. "Manners Maketh Man: Living, Dining and Becoming a Man in the Later Middle Ages." In *Rites of Passage: Cultures of Transition in the Fourteenth Century*. Edited by Nicola F. McDonald and W. M. Ormrod, 67-81. Woodbridge: York Medieval Press, 2004.